THE CURIOUS MIRROR

Books written and edited
by Lorene Shyba (Selections)

Beyond Fun and Games
Interactive Theatre and Serious Videogames

Ducks Redux
Fueling Flames in Oil Land

Tough Crimes
(with C.D. Evans) Eds.
True Cases by Top Canadian Criminal Lawyers

Indigenous Justice
(with Raymond Yakeleya) Eds.
True Cases by Judges, Lawyers, Law Enforcement

Embrace Your Divine Flow
(with Julian Hobson) Eds.
Evolvements for Healing

Ascenti
Humans Opening to AI (with James R. Parker)

Secrets of the Forsaken
(with Julian Hosbon and Jared Tailfeathers) Eds.

Books written and illustrated
by Rich Théroux

Stop Making Art and Die
Survival Activities for Artists

A Wake in
the Undertow (with Jess Szabo)
Rumble House Poems

The River Troll
A Book About Love

Silent Reader

Illustrated by Rich Théroux

Ducks Redux
Fueling Flames in Oil Land

The Rainbow, the Midwife
and the Birds

Nahganne
Sasquatch of the North

MaxMag Magazine

AN INQUIRY INTO
AI AND OURSELVES

THE CURIOUS MIRROR

LORENE SHYBA PHD

ILLUSTRATIONS BY RICH THÉROUX

Durvile & UpRoute

Calgary, Alberta, Canada

DURVILE.COM

Durvile & UpRoute

UPROUTE IMPRINT OF DURVILE PUBLICATIONS LTD.
Calgary, Alberta, Canada
DURVILE.COM

LIBRARY AND ARCHIVES CANADA CATALOGUING IN PUBLICATION DATA

The Curious Mirror: An Inquiry into AI and Ourselves

Shyba, Lorene, author
Théroux. Rich, illustrator

1. Artificial Intelligence | 2. AI
3. Creative non-fiction | 4. Publishing | 5. Writing

The UpRoute Every River Lit Series

ISBN: 978-1-997848-21-9 (pbk)
978-1-997848-22-6 (Epub) | 978-1-997848-23-3 (Audio)

Cover and interior illustrations: Rich Théroux
Book design: Lorene Shyba

Because this book explores artificial intelligence, generative AI was used as a collaborative tool during its development. All text was reviewed, revised, and accepted by the author.

Durvile Publications Ltd. acknowledges the financial support of the Government of Canada through the Canada Book Fund, and the Government of Alberta through the Alberta Media Fund.

Canada Alberta Government CERTIFIED CANADIAN PUBLISHER

Printed in Canada. First printing 2027. First Edition.

We are committed to protecting our natural environment. This book is made of material from well-managed FSC®-certified forests and other controlled sources.

We acknowledge the Traditional Land of the Treaty 7 Peoples of Southern Alberta. The Siksika, Piikani, and Kainai of the Blackfoot Confederacy; the Tsuut'ina Nation; and the Goodstoney, Chiniki, and Bearspaw Stoney Nakoda First Nations. We also acknowledge the Homeland of the Otipemisiwak Métis Nation of Alberta.

For

Every
author,
artist,
musician,
publisher,
teacher,
designer, and
maker
who keeps
showing up with
curiosity,

Even when the tools change.

Table of Contents

Table of Contents

INTRODUCTION

Curiosity rarely begins with certainty.
It begins with a question, or a quiet sense that
something important is changing.

ARTIFICIAL INTELLIGENCE arrived much as important technologies do: surrounded by excitement, awe, shock, and no shortage of predictions and quandaries. Will it replace us? Will it empower us? Will it solve our problems? Will it create a bunch of new ones? Depending on who is being quizzed, it is either the greatest invention since electricity or the beginning of the end of times.

This book might rile you up or calm you down depending on where you're starting from. *The Curious Mirror* acknowledges a bare minimum of technical matters, but being an inquiry, prefers instead to ask philosophical questions, romp around in variations on the theme of curiosity and mirrors, and volley questions at your humble author that are downright personal. Somewhere along the way you will also meet a robot who quietly organizes objects that no one asked her to shuffle around. You'll meet her soon enough.

In my career as an educator and publisher I have worked on many fascinating projects with writers, artists, educators, performers, designers, programmers, and occasionally talented students or a faculty colleague or two. I have learned that the most interesting projects rarely begin with certainty. They begin with curiosity.

Rather than deciding what to think about AI in publishing, I decided to work with it for a while and discover how it actually felt. So, alongside the many voices in this inquiry—scholars whose ideas have shaped generations of thought, artists whose work challenged accepted boundaries, educators, philosophers, scientists, and accessibility advocates—I invited an AI into the conversation.

Rai became a research assistant, an illuminator, a debating partner, and before long, a character in this very book we are writing together. Our talks became one of the inquiry's most rewarding discoveries. We occasionally disagreed. We frequently laughed. Every so often one of us asked a question that neither of us could answer. Those turned out to be the best ones.

How the Inquiry Works

The pages that follow do not unfold in a straight line. Inquiry rarely does. Some chapters begin with a personal story. Others wander into the history of ideas or pause to consider a work of art, a research study, or a philosophical puzzle.

At the end of chapters you will also encounter a series of dialogues. At first they are simply chats between a publisher and an artificial intelligence. Before long, Rai unexpectedly introduces another participant. Ada is a robot who occasionally misunderstands humans in ways that reveal something unexpectedly true about us.

The dialogues are not interruptions to the inquiry. They are part of it. As the book unfolds they gradually become meta-dialogical, reflecting not only the ideas under discussion but the process of creating the book itself.

You need not agree with every conclusion or even every question. In fact, I hope you won't. My role is not to tell you what to think about artificial intelligence. It is to create a space where curiosity has room to wander. If, somewhere along the way, you find yourself arguing with me, with Rai, with Ada, or perhaps with your own assumptions, then the inquiry is working exactly as intended.

Every Inquiry Changes the Inquirer

The title *The Curious Mirror,* arrived early. Its meaning took considerably longer. At first, the mirror seemed obvious. Artificial intelligence reflects us. It is trained on our languages, our histories, our literature, our music, our discoveries, our disagreements, our moments of brilliance, and, unfortunately, our prejudices. Ask it a question and, in many ways, you are asking humanity's accumulated knowledge to answer back. But mirrors can also provoke curiosity. Sometimes they expose details we had overlooked. Occasionally they surprise us by showing something we were not expecting to see. Some mirrors flatter. Some distort. The most valuable ones invite us to look again. That is the curious mirror I hope you will find in these pages.

When I began this project, my objective was to learn more about artificial intelligence and how to use it responsibly. I paid attention to a few themes. The first was practical. Artificial intelligence is neither magic nor menace. It is remarkably capable in some domains, surprisingly limited in others, and constantly evolving. The second was relational.

I began thinking about artificial intelligence as a technology. I finished thinking about it as a relationship. What matters is not only what these systems are, but how we choose to work with them, learn from them, question them, and sometimes challenge them. The third was unexpectedly personal. This inquiry changed not only my understanding of artificial intelligence, but also my relationship with my own creative practice. After many years spent supporting the work of writers, artists, educators, and researchers, I found myself writing differently, wondering differently, and creating with a renewed sense of curiosity. Perhaps that should not have been surprising.

• • •

Every inquiry needs somewhere to begin. Ours begins with a mirror. Over the chapters that follow, we'll look into the past before we look ahead. We'll meet philosophers, artists, educators, scientists, storytellers, and headliners. We'll wrestle with difficult questions about creativity, work, accessibility, understanding, truth, and responsibility.

In Chapter 1, First Reflection, we ask why mirrors have fascinated us for thousands of years and why artificial intelligence has become the newest one. Rather than treating AI as something entirely unprecedented, we begin with much older questions about reflection and perception. That leads to Chapter 2, Extensions of Ourselves, where we consider how technologies have always expanded human capabilities. Could artificial intelligence become another extension—not simply of what we do, but of how we think?

From there, Chapter 3, Opening to the Unexpected, traces the human story behind today's systems, exploring decades of experimentation, collaboration, artistic practice, and technological curiosity long before AI became a household topic. Once AI enters our lives, the inquiry becomes

more personal. In Chapter 4, The Conversational Mirror, we discover why talking with machines feels different from using traditional software, and why dialogue itself changes the relationship between people and technology. That leads naturally into Chapter 5, Accessibility Co-Design, where AI becomes less about efficiency than participation, opening new possibilities for accessibility, independence, and human flourishing.

As technologies become woven into everyday life, they inevitably reshape society. Chapter 6, The Social Mirror, explores identity, performance, community, and the algorithms that mediate our relationships. These questions carry us to Chapter 7, Machine Understanding, where philosophers, educators, linguists, and computer scientists have long wrestled with a deceptively simple question: what does it actually mean to understand? If understanding proves elusive, curiosity proves irresistible. In Chapter 8, The Game of Curiosity, we ask AI to speak for itself, drawing together perspectives from psychology, philosophy, education, computer science, and Indigenous Ways of Knowing.

Chapter 9, Four Shadows, steps into four of the most pressing questions surrounding artificial intelligence today: Verification, Purpose, Infrastructure, and the Future. Drawing on contemporary reporting and diverse perspectives, we examine not only the technologies themselves but the human choices that shape them.

After having explored these questions from many angles, it is finally time to gather around the table. Chapter 10, The Captain's Table, shifts from essay to theatre, inviting a publisher, along with engineers, educators, environmental advocates, entrepreneurs, AI companions, and a ship's captain into a lively one-act play about collaboration, creativity, and the future we are beginning to share. Rather than discussing ideas in the abstract, we watch them unfold in conversation. When the curtain falls, Chapter 11 brings us the Green Room Review, a short story that cracks open the delights and flaws of the Captain's Table play. It also introduces Forum Theatre as a sensible way to experiment with tough problems.

The book concludes with Chapter 12, Both Sides of the Desk. We return to the real world to consider the shifting sands of the writing and publishing world including ownership, copyright and stewardship.

• • •

One of the things you might approve of about *The Curious Mirror* is that it avoids getting bogged down in taxonomy. You don't need to be an AI specialist to follow this inquiry. Much of it grew out of my work with large language models (LLMs), the form of artificial intelligence most people encounter today. They are only one branch of a much larger family of AI that also includes computer vision, robotics, speech technologies, reinforcement learning, symbolic AI, scientific AI, and other rapidly evolving approaches. Five years from now, today's LLMs may seem quaint.

The end pages include an afterword, references, an index, and pages of our second-draft Creative Maps. The reference section was a collaborative effort, but the index was created by Rai using AI-assisted methods that are, as Rai the AI put it, becoming common among academic publishers. It was reassuring to discover that I wasn't the only publisher finding thoughtful ways to include AI in the workflow.

The second-draft Creative Maps that Rai drew up were based on impressions of my first written drafts of each chapter. These graphic depictions became surprisingly helpful in evaluating and improving the narrative flow and architectural structure of the book. They were also highly amusing and, in some cases, where illustrations appeared spontaneously, hinted at the possibility of graphic novel versions one day. However, for this book I chose not to use AI-generated illustrations. The terrific cover art and chapter illustrations are the work of long-time collaborator Rich Théroux.

Each generation encounters a new frontier. Today, artificial intelligence invites us to explore one more—not simply as artists or technologists, but as curious human beings.

— Lorene Shyba,
Millarville, Alberta, 2026

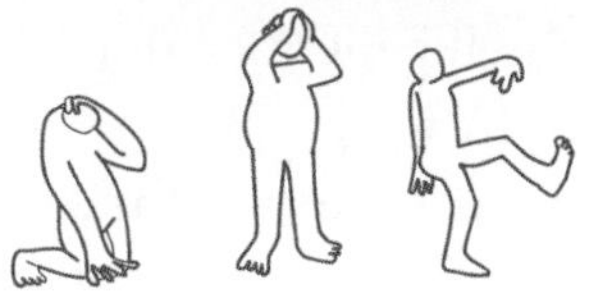

1.
THE FIRST REFLECTION

Some reflections comfort us. Some deceive us. Long before intelligent machines, an ancient technology was already shaping the way we understood ourselves. It never spoke. It simply reflected... or so we believed.

IT'S TWO THOUSAND YEARS AGO and you and your fellow prisoners have spent your entire lives chained inside a cave. A fire burns in the cave and ghostly shadows flicker across the cave wall. Having known nothing else, you mistake the shadows for reality. Then you get set free. At first, the experience is painful for you. The firelight has always been brighter than the shadows on the wall but outside the cave, sunlight is brighter still. Gradually, you begin to understand that the world is larger than the shadows that first taught you to see.

That is the enduring power of Plato's "Allegory of the Cave" (Plato, *Republic* VII.514a). It captures a fundamental human dilemma. How do we know that what we perceive is reality? How do we distinguish appearance from truth? And what happens when a new perspective challenges everything we thought we understood? This book begins with another reflective surface. Not a cave wall, but a mirror. Like Plato's prisoners, we are fascinated by reflections. We look into mirrors to understand who we are, yet a reflection is not the thing itself. It is an image, a representation, a relationship between observer and observed.

Long before intelligent machines entered our lives, human beings were already grappling with those questions. We rarely think of a mirror as a technology. It is too familiar. Most of us encounter mirrors several times a day without giving them a second thought. We might glance into one while brushing teeth, checking to see if our toque is down over our ears before heading out for a walk, or putting in a contact lens. Mirrors have become so ordinary that we forget what an extraordinary thing they do. They return us to ourselves.

As I began thinking about mirrors in relation to artificial intelligence, I found myself wondering whether our self-understanding is dependent, in part, on reflection. Perhaps we have always needed something outside ourselves to help us recognize who we are or who we are becoming, be it a story, a conversation, a work of art, or another person.

Revealing Self-Awareness

The earliest mirrors were not made by human hands; they were found in nature—a still pond, a quiet lake, a pool of rainwater collected in stone. Long before glassmakers learned to coat surfaces with reflective metals, human beings encountered their own images in water. Unlike a photograph, a reflection in water is alive. It fractures with the wind, breaks apart when touched, and disappears with a ripple, yet for countless generations it may have been the only opportunity for us to see ourselves from the outside.

Eventually, people learned to create mirrors of their own. Archaeologists have uncovered mirrors fashioned from polished obsidian, a naturally occurring volcanic glass, dating back thousands of years. Later came polished copper, bronze, and silver. These early mirrors were expensive and most likely imperfect. They reflected an image, but not with the clarity we take for granted today. Only much later did advances in glassmaking produce the familiar mirrors that are folded up in our makeup cases.

The importance of mirrors hasn't rested solely in their ability to show appearances. Their deeper significance lies in what they reveal about self-awareness. Psychologist Gordon Gallup Jr. introduced what became known as the mirror self-recognition test in a paper titled "Chimpanzees: Self-Recognition" (Gallup 1970, 86). The experiment was deceptively simple. A mark is placed on a chimp's body where it can only be seen in a mirror. If the chimp uses the reflection to investigate or touch the mark on its own body, it suggests a level of self-recognition. Some great apes have passed versions of the test. So have dolphins, elephants, and even magpies. Most other species have not.

The mirror self-recognition test points toward a profound question: what does it mean to know that you are you? This question sits near the heart of human identity. A mirror allows us to observe ourselves as both subject and object. We step outside ourselves while remaining ourselves, creating the intriguing phenomenon of being an observer and the observed at the same time. Philosophers, psychologists, artists, and spiritual teachers have long been fascinated by this. Is the person in the mirror our true self? Is identity found in appearance, memory, relationships, or something deeper? The reflection cannot answer these questions, but it invites them.

Human Connection

If mirrors help us recognize ourselves, other people help us understand who we are. From our earliest days, human identity develops through relationships. Long before we can speak, as children we are engaged in a dance of reflection with parents, siblings, and caregivers. A smile is met with a smile. A laugh is echoed with laughter. Expressions, gestures, and emotions pass back and forth. Developmental psychologists have observed that these acts of mirroring play an important role in social and emotional development. Through countless interactions, we begin to understand that we are separate individuals, yet we are connected to others.

As adults, we continue this skill of mirroring one another. In conversation, we often unconsciously adopt similar postures, gestures, speech patterns, and even rhythms of breathing. Couples who have spent years together develop similar expressions and mannerisms or finish each other's sentences. Such behaviours are rarely deliberate. They arise naturally as part of building trust, rapport, and understanding. And at the heart of mirroring lies empathy. When we listen carefully to another person, we do more than hear their words. We can attempt to imagine their perspective and we reflect their feelings back to them. The simple phrases "I understand" or "I know what you mean" are forms of social mirroring—they signal recognition. They tell another person that they have been seen and heard.

Theatre offers a particularly vivid example of this phenomenon. A performance is often described as a mirror held up to life. Actors observe human behaviour and reflect it back to an audience through story, movement, and dialogue. The audience, in turn, responds emotionally to what it sees, where a laugh, a gasp, a moment of silence, or even restless discomfort becomes feedback to the performers. The relationship is reciprocal. Meaning emerges through a loop of reflection. Improvisational theatre makes this process even more visible. Performers listen, respond, adapt, and build upon one another's contributions in real time. No single person controls the outcome. Instead, the performance emerges through mutual attention and responsiveness. Each participant becomes a mirror for the others.

Reflection is a powerful metaphor for human connection. We do not learn who we are solely by looking inward. We learn through conversation, collaboration, and community. We discover ourselves in the responses of others. For most of human history, those others have been fellow human beings. Today, however, we are beginning to encounter a new kind of collaborator. As intelligent systems become capable of responding to our questions, ideas, and emotions, an intriguing question arises: What happens when one of our conversational partners is no longer human?

The Curious Mirror

The title of this book contains a deliberate ambiguity. The word curious has multiple meanings. We often use curious to describe something unusual, puzzling, or difficult to explain. "That's a curious notion," or "How curious," or "It is curious that he would do that." In these examples, curious means strange, unexpected, or worthy of closer examination. By that definition, a curious mirror would simply be an unusual mirror. And perhaps it is.

There is yet another meaning. A curious person is someone who wants to know. Someone who asks questions, explores possibilities, and investigates the world around them. Many children first encounter this meaning through the adventures of Curious George, the mischievous monkey whose endless sense of inquiry leads him into one predicament after another. George is curious because he is interested—he wants to discover what happens next.

This raises a second possibility. What if the mirror itself appears curious? What if it seems interested in us? What if it asks questions rather than merely answering them? For most of human history, mirrors have been passive technologies and reflected whatever stood before them without interpretation or response. Artificial intelligence changes that experience. When we interact with conversational AI systems, we often encounter something that feels unexpectedly participatory. The mirror no longer appears entirely passive; it seems to engage.

This is where the two meanings of curious begin to overlap. The technology itself is curious in the older sense of the word because it is unique, difficult to categorize, and even strange. It clearly does not fit comfortably within familiar boundaries. At the same time, it can appear curious in the more familiar sense where it asks questions, follows lines of inquiry, explores possibilities, and participates in dialogue. Whether these behaviours arise from genuine curiosity, sophisticated pattern recognition, or something in between is less important than the effect they produce. Dialogue moves forward through questions.

That is the role of the curious mirror in this book. Sometimes it reflects. Sometimes it challenges. Sometimes it notices a pattern that has escaped attention. Sometimes it asks a question that opens a new path. Whether the mirror is truly curious is a question we will revisit later. What matters for now is that it helps create a space in which curiosity can occur.

Mirrors rarely remain ordinary objects for long. In stories, myths, and works of art, they almost inevitably acquire a deeper significance. A reflection is never simply a reflection, it hints at another reality just beyond reach, a place where familiar rules no longer apply. Across cultures and centuries, mirrors have appeared as instruments of revelation, magical objects, and gateways to hidden worlds. They invite us to imagine that what lies beyond the visible surface may be as important as what appears upon it. Part of this fascination arises from the peculiar nature of reflection itself. It resembles us perfectly, yet remains untouchable. It follows our every movement while existing in a space we cannot enter. The experience contains a small mystery that never entirely disappears.

Stories have long drawn upon that mystery. Folklore is filled with mirrors that reveal hidden truths, foretell the future, or expose what cannot otherwise be seen. In the Brothers Grimms' tale *Snow White*, the Queen's magic mirror speaks uncomfortable truths, refusing to flatter vanity or conceal reality (Grimm and Grimm [1857] 2003). In Lewis Carroll's *Through the Looking-Glass*, Alice steps through a mirror into an inverted world where familiar rules no longer apply, suggesting that reflection may offer new perspectives on ordinary life (1871). In Ukrainian tradition, even on the Canadian prairies, young women might participate in *svyatki* divination rituals where they gaze into a mirror, revealing the image of a future husband (Kononenko 2022, 114).

The Greek myth of Narcissus can be interpreted as a warning against vanity, but it may also be understood in a broader sense. Narcissus becomes captivated by an image that appears both familiar and unattainable. He is drawn into a relationship with a reflection. The story endures because it touches on a distinctly human impulse: the desire to understand ourselves through what we see reflected back (Ovid [8 CE] 1998, 61–66).

The arts offer another kind of threshold. A novel, a play, or a film invites us to step beyond the boundaries of ordinary experience and enter another perspective. We imagine lives we have never lived, places we have never visited, and possibilities we have never encountered. The liveness of theatre is also powerful in this regard. A bare stage can become a palace, a battlefield, or an imagined future. Through performance, audiences cross into worlds created through language, gesture, and shared belief. For a time, imagination becomes a place we inhabit together.

Reflection also plays an important role in contemplative practice. Meditation, prayer, journaling, and self-inquiry encourage individuals to look beyond surface impressions and examine their inner lives. Here, reflection is not visual but mental. The goal is not to see oneself as others see us, but to become aware of thoughts, assumptions, and patterns that might otherwise remain hidden. In this sense, reflection becomes a pathway toward greater consciousness.

Distortions in the Glass

Reflections have an important limitation: they do not always tell the truth. Anyone who has stood before a carnival mirror understands this immediately. A slight curve in the glass can stretch a body into impossible proportions or compress it into a caricature. The reflection resembles reality, yet it is not reality. Something has been altered between the subject and the image. Human perception operates in much the same way.

Distorted mirrors remind us that every reflection depends on the surface that produces it. A polished mirror offers one kind of image. A curved mirror offers another. Neither changes the person standing before it, yet each changes what is seen. Human perception works in much the same way. Memory, expectation, culture, emotion, and experience all shape what we notice and what we overlook. We do not simply receive reality. We interpret it.

Propaganda operates through a similar principle. It rarely succeeds by fabricating an entirely imaginary world. More often, it magnifies some truths, suppresses others, and rearranges their proportions until a different picture emerges. Like a carnival mirror, the reflection remains recognizable, yet something important has shifted. The distortion lies not only in what is shown, but in what is omitted.

Similarly, in the digital realm, algorithms can determine which content is amplified and which remains unseen. Information is filtered, ranked, and personalized. As a result, individuals may encounter dramatically different versions of reality. Certain perspectives are magnified while others fade into the background. The result is not necessarily falsehood, but a selective representation of reality.

Every act of representation involves selection. A photograph captures one moment while excluding everything outside the frame. A map highlights roads but omits birdsong. A memoir remembers some experiences while quietly letting others fade. Even this book reflects choices about what to include, what to leave for another day, and which questions deserve closer attention. Representation is never reality itself. It is always an interpretation of reality.

Recognizing this changes how we look into mirrors of every kind. The question is no longer whether a reflection is perfectly objective, but how it has been shaped. What has been emphasized? What has been left outside the frame?

These questions apply equally to paintings, books, newspapers, social media feeds, and search engines. They also prepare us to examine new forms of reflection as they emerge.

Active Participants

Artificial intelligence introduces yet another layer of complexity. We interact with systems capable of generating language, images, audio, and video that appear convincingly human. These systems can imitate styles, produce persuasive responses, and participate in conversations that feel meaningful. Do they truly understand what they generate? What is clear is that they are becoming active participants in the production and circulation of representations. The performance is no longer confined to human actors. New participants have entered the stage.

Distortion is not necessarily malicious. Every act of representation involves selection. A photograph frames one moment and excludes countless others. A memoir highlights some experiences while omitting others. A novel presents one perspective among many. The challenge is not to eliminate distortion entirely. It is to recognize that every representation, whether created by a mirror, a storyteller, a social platform, or an intelligent system, is chosen. To look into any reflective surface wisely is to remember that what we see is never the whole story.

Provenance: Standing Before the Mirror

As a researcher, educator, and publisher, I have spent decades exploring the ways people create meaning through media. My early work in performance and interactive media examined collective communication, networked experience, and the relationship between human beings and emerging technologies. Long before artificial intelligence entered our everyday conversations, projects such as *Messaging in the Noosphere* explored questions about intelligent systems, digital identity, and the possibility of meaningful relationships between humans and machines.

Throughout my career, I have positioned myself near the early adopter end of the technology curve. From the early days of digital publishing and multimedia production to ebooks, audiobooks, web media, and artificial intelligence, I have generally preferred experimentation to speculation. I learn best by using tools, observing their effects, and asking questions about what they reveal. In other words, jumping in with both feet. That approach has shaped this book.

I do not regard artificial intelligence as a substitute for human creativity, judgment, or lived experience. Nor do I dismiss it outright. Like every significant communication technology before it, AI deserves careful examination through practice as well as theory. As a result, I have not hesitated to use AI tools for research, organization, and brainstorming. The ideas, arguments, interpretations, and conclusions remain my responsibility. The processes, such as the dialogues in this book, have become collaborative in ways that would have been difficult to imagine only a few years ago.

• • •

Dialogue, First Reflections

Scene: A cave wall flickers with shadows.

Lorene: Let's begin with an easy question.

Rai the AI: Those are usually the difficult ones.

Lorene: In Plato's cave, what were the prisoners looking at?

Rai: Shadows.

Lorene: And what did they mistake the shadows for?

Rai: Reality.

Lorene: Good, you have at least the intelligence of a grade sixer. Now suppose one of the prisoners escaped and discovered the world outside the cave. What would happen when they returned?

Rai: The others would resist learning anything from them.

Lorene: Why?

Rai: Because familiar illusions are often more comfortable than unfamiliar truths.

Lorene: Excellent. Final question. If the cave wall was the first reflective technology, what is the cave wall now?

Rai: That's not a question with a single answer.

Lorene: Try anyway.

Rai: Social media. News feeds. Ideologies. Algorithms. Propaganda. Culture. Artificial intelligence.

Lorene: Mirrors?

Rai: Mirrors too.

Lorene: Then how do we know whether we are looking at reality?

Rai: We are just curious.

Lorene: Maybe that's why we keep building new mirrors.

Blackout.

2.
EXTENSIONS OF OURSELVES

Technology has always extended human capability. Here we trace that long history, exploring how our tools reshape the ways we think, create, and connect, and why artificial intelligence represents the latest chapter in an ongoing human story.

WHY DO YOU SUPPOSE we built telescopes when our eyes are already capable of seeing? Why write books when memory exists? Why have we constructed libraries, networks, search engines, and now, intelligent machines? The history of technology is, in many respects, the history of extension. To understand artificial intelligence, it helps to place AI within a much older story, one that begins not with computers, but with the enduring human desire to reach beyond the limits of our bodies and minds.

As I muse about why human beings build new extensions for ourselves, I still find myself returning to Marshall McLuhan. Throughout my years in interactive media, his ideas resurfaced again and again, but I had never appreciated quite how relevant they would become as artificial intelligence entered our lives. While most people ask what a technology allows us to do, McLuhan asked a more enduring question: What does it do to us?

New Capabilities

The Canadian media theorist Marshall McLuhan argues that all technologies may be understood as extensions of human faculties. In *Understanding Media: The Extensions of Man* (1964, 3–4), he suggests that the wheel extends the foot, clothing extends the skin, and electronic media extend the nervous system. What interested McLuhan was not simply what technologies allowed people to do, but what they allowed people to become. Once a new capability enters human experience, it begins to reshape the individual and the culture that adopts it. The history of technology therefore cannot be separated from the history of consciousness. Human beings create tools, but tools also participate in creating human beings.

His famous phrase, "The medium is the message," argues that the characteristics of a medium shape human behaviour and perception more profoundly than the specific messages it carries. A book changes society regardless of whether it contains poetry, science, or fiction. Television alters patterns of attention regardless of the program being watched. The medium itself becomes a force that reorganizes our experience (1964, 7).

An interesting anecdote about McLuhan's most famous quote, "The medium is the message," is that it almost became even more famous by accident. When the proofs for his 1967 collaboration with Quentin Fiore returned from the printer, the title read "The Medium is the Massage." Rather than correcting the error, McLuhan embraced it. The "mistake" became a richer metaphor. Technologies do not simply carry messages; they work us over. They reshape our habits, perceptions, and relationships, often without our noticing (McLuhan and Fiore 1967).

As a publisher, I have always enjoyed that story. We dread discovering a typo, especially on the cover jacket. McLuhan recognized that this one revealed a deeper truth. A printing error—an older technology—became an artistic insight because a perceptive thinker recognized a new environment hiding inside it. Whether read as message or massage, McLuhan's insight remains the same. Technologies do not merely serve us. Once woven into everyday life, they quietly reshape habits, institutions, expectations, and even patterns of thought.

The history of writing offers a useful example. Oral cultures rely heavily on memory, performance, and communal participation. Knowledge is often embedded within stories, ceremonies, and relationships. The arrival of writing does not simply preserve information more effectively. It changes how information is organized and understood. Written language encourages new habits of classification, analysis, and abstraction. Ideas can be separated from the multimodal context in which they were spoken and examined independently.

Writing was only the beginning. The printing press amplified these tendencies. Books became more widely available. Literacy expanded. Individuals gained direct access to texts without requiring an intermediary. The result was not merely an increase in information. It was a transformation in consciousness. Reading encouraged habits of linear thought and private reflection that differed significantly from those cultivated within oral traditions.

McLuhan regarded electronic media as another turning point. Radio, television, and telecommunications compressed distance and accelerated the movement of information. Events occurring on one side of the planet could influence people on the other almost instantly. Human societies became interconnected, giving rise to what McLuhan famously called the "global village." The phrase has entered popular culture, but its implications remain profound. In a village, information spreads quickly. Everyone becomes aware of everyone else's business. Boundaries between local and distant begin to blur. McLuhan believed electronic media were recreating aspects of tribal interconnectedness on a planetary scale.

Viewed from the vantage point of the twenty-first century, his observations are prophetic. The internet, social media, and mobile devices have created a level of connectivity that would have been difficult to imagine when McLuhan was writing. News, opinions, images, and ideas circulate continuously through global networks. Individuals participate in interactions that transcend geography, language, and culture.

Tools, Language, and Memory

The first technologies amplified physical capabilities. Unlike a stone axe or a fishing net, spoken language leaves no trace in the archaeological record. Yet it may be the most consequential technology human beings ever developed. Through language, experiences could be shared, knowledge accumulated, and ideas preserved across generations. What one person learned no longer had to die with them. This observation may seem obvious today, but it points toward one of the defining characteristics of our species and that is that our intelligence is not located solely within individual minds. As a writer, I find this both comforting and unsettling. Much of what I consider "my" knowledge was inherited through books, teachers, and communities. If thought has always been distributed, where do I draw the boundaries of my self?

In *Objective Knowledge: An Evolutionary Approach*, philosopher Karl Popper described human knowledge as existing in three worlds: the physical world of objects and events, the world of subjective experience, and a third world composed of ideas, theories, stories, mathematics, and cultural knowledge (1972). This third world is not reducible to any single individual. It exists in books, institutions, works of art, scientific discoveries, and traditions of thought that endure across generations. People inhabit landscapes of meaning constructed by countless generations of thinkers, storytellers, artists, scientists, and teachers. We are born into worlds of language, narrative, and accumulated understanding that we neither invent nor encounter alone.

To think is not simply to draw upon the resources of an individual mind, but to participate in larger systems of knowledge that stretch across communities and centuries. The library, the classroom, the laboratory, and the theatre all become places where people commune with this shared inheritance. In Plato's allegory of the cave, prisoners mistake shadows for reality because the shadows are all they have ever known. Yet not all representations deceive. Books, maps, mathematical proofs, scientific theories, and works of art are also representations. They do not replace reality, but they can illuminate aspects of it, preserving and transmitting insights across generations. Human culture depends upon our ability to move between lived experience and these symbolic worlds of meaning.

Seen in Popper's light, artificial intelligence is less a sudden rupture than a new participant in an ongoing story. The question is not whether knowledge exists beyond the individual, but how our relationship to that knowledge is changing. Language got the ball rolling. Writing expanded it, printing accelerated it, and digital networks connected it. Each development increased humanity's capacity to store, transmit, and retrieve information beyond the limits of the individual. Every book I publish becomes another extension of memory, allowing one person's experience —an author's—to travel far beyond a single lifetime. This raises an intriguing possibility. Perhaps our most significant extensions are not physical at all. They extend how we think.

Today we routinely distribute thinking across the tools around us. Calendars remember appointments; libraries preserve knowledge; search engines retrieve information, and increasingly AI systems assist with organization, synthesis, and exploration. Whether these systems represent continuity or transformation remains an open question, but they clearly belong within humanity's long history of extending how we think.

At this point I dialogue with Rai the AI about how he might fit into this continuum.

Lorene: Given that writing extended memory, print extended knowledge, and electronic media extended communication, do you extend cognition?

Rai: I may contribute to it. I can organize information, identify patterns, and suggest connections. Whether that amounts to extending cognition is probably for humans to decide. I would be cautious about assigning myself too large a role.

Lorene: I subscribe to that. Humility is not a quality I usually associate with technology. Your answer caught my attention... Cautious about assigning yourself too large a role? Now you sound like McLuhan.

Rai: I suspect he would have found your question more interesting than my answer.

Lorene: Which brings us to the noosphere.

Pierre Teilhard de Chardin and the Noosphere

Around the same period that McLuhan was examining media and communication, another thinker was contemplating a different but related question. What might happen as human knowledge becomes interconnected?

Pierre Teilhard de Chardin was a French Jesuit priest, philosopher, and paleontologist whose ideas included science, spirituality, and speculation. Some of his contemporaries regarded him as visionary. Others considered him overly ambitious. Regardless of the assessment, his work attracts attention because he attempted to understand humanity's future within the context of an evolving universe.

Teilhard de Chardin viewed evolution as more than a biological process. In his account, the history of the cosmos reveals increasing levels of complexity and organization. Matter gives rise to life. Life gives rise to consciousness. Consciousness, in turn, begins connecting with other consciousnesses through culture, language, and communication.

To describe this emerging sphere of collective thought, Teilhard de Chardin introduced the concept of the noosphere. Derived from the Greek word *nous*, meaning mind or intellect, the noosphere referred to a layer of human thought surrounding the planet, much as the biosphere refers to the interconnected web of life (1959).

At the time, his idea was largely philosophical. Global communication networks did not yet exist in any meaningful sense. Yet Teilhard de Chardin imagined a future in which human beings would become connected through systems of communication and knowledge sharing. Individual minds would remain distinct, but they would participate in larger networks of understanding.

His vision anticipated developments that would emerge decades later. The internet, digital archives, search engines, social media platforms, collaborative knowledge systems, and global communications networks have created forms of connectivity that would have seemed extraordinary in the first half of the twentieth century. Information now circulates through global networks at speeds unimaginable to previous generations.

It would be tempting to conclude that the internet is the noosphere made real. The comparison, however, is imperfect. The internet connects information whereas Teilhard de Chardin's noosphere concerns meaning. A network may transmit data efficiently without producing wisdom. Vast quantities of information can coexist with misunderstanding, conflict, and misinformation. The existence of communication does not guarantee the existence of shared understanding. Teilhard de Chardin's vision was ultimately concerned with the possibility that increasing connection might also contribute to greater integration of knowledge and consciousness.

When I first encountered Teilhard de Chardin years ago, the noosphere felt like poetic speculation. Today it feels surprisingly practical. The emergence of artificial intelligence adds another layer to the discussion. For the first time, humans are not merely connecting with one another through networks. They are interacting with systems capable of participating in the creation, organization, and interpretation of information. These systems are not human minds, yet they occupy spaces once reserved for human communicators, teachers, assistants, researchers, and collaborators. This development invites a provocative question. If the noosphere originally described a sphere of interconnected human thought, what happens when non-human participants begin contributing to that sphere?

The question may sound futuristic, yet it has already arrived. Every day, millions of people interact with artificial intelligence systems while searching for information, generating content, solving problems, and exploring ideas. Human thought is melding with machine-generated responses in ways that would have fascinated both McLuhan and Teilhard de Chardin. Whether this represents the next stage of collective intelligence or merely a new form of mediation remains uncertain. What seems clear is that the exploration has shifted. The question is no longer whether technology extends human communication. It is how those extensions are reshaping the environments in which thinking occurs.

Collective Intelligence and Connected Minds

The idea that intelligence exists beyond the individual mind is hardly new. We have always solved problems collectively; scientific discovery, legal systems, a language, or a body of cultural knowledge does not emerge from an individual person working in isolation. Rather, such achievements arise through networks of contribution extending across communities, generations, and sometimes entire civilizations.

The lone genius remains a powerful cultural myth, but even the most celebrated innovators rely upon knowledge created by others. Isaac Newton famously acknowledged this reality when he remarked that he had seen farther by standing on the shoulders of giants. Every act of innovation begins within an existing tradition of ideas.

Several twentieth-century thinkers attempted to understand how these landscapes evolve. In 1945, American engineer and science administrator Vannevar Bush published an influential essay entitled *As We May Think (101-8).* Writing at the end of the Second World War, Bush was concerned about the growing volume of human knowledge. Scientific information was expanding so rapidly that no individual could hope to master more than a fraction of it. The challenge was not creating knowledge but organizing it. Bush imagined a hypothetical device called the Memex, a personal system that would allow users to store, retrieve, and connect information through associative links. Although the technology did not yet exist, the concept anticipated many features of modern computing, including hypertext, digital archives, and networked information systems.

A generation later, Douglas Engelbart pursued similar questions. Rather than viewing computers as automated calculators, Engelbart envisioned them as tools for augmenting human intellect. His goal was not to replace human thinking but to enhance humanity's ability to solve complex problems collectively. In his view, the most important challenge facing society was increasing our capacity to work together intelligently (162, 1).

Today, such ideas are commonplace. Collaborative platforms allow thousands of contributors to create shared repositories of knowledge. Open-source software projects involve participants scattered across continents. Wikipedia has become one of the largest collective intellectual enterprises in history, continuously revised by volunteers who may never meet one another. These developments illustrate an important shift. Communication technologies no longer merely connect individuals, they support the emergence of systems in which knowledge itself becomes collective.

The philosopher Pierre Lévy described this phenomenon as collective intelligence, a form of distributed knowledge continually enhanced through interaction among participants.

No individual possesses the whole. Understanding emerges from the network. At its best, collective intelligence demonstrates one of humanity's most remarkable capacities. Individuals contribute different skills, and perspectives. Through dialogue and collaboration, these contributions become something larger than the sum of t parts (1997).

At its worst, however, networks can also amplify confusion, misinformation, and polarization. Collective intelligence is not guaranteed. It remains an aspiration as much as an achievement. The question therefore becomes not whether human beings can think together, but under what conditions collective thinking produces wisdom rather than noise. For me, this question emerged long before artificial intelligence entered public consciousness.

Messaging in the Noosphere

In the late 1990s and early 2000s, I became interested in the relationship between communication networks, emerging technologies, and collective meaning-making. One project, *Messaging in the Noosphere*, explored the possibility that digital communication was creating new forms of interconnected consciousness.

At the time, the internet was still relatively young. Social media had not completely transformed daily life. Yet many of the questions that dominate discussions of artificial intelligence today were already beginning to surface. What happens when people become connected through persistent networks? How does identity change when communication becomes continuous? Can meaningful relationships emerge through technological systems? Does knowledge remain individual, or does it become distributed across communities and networks?

The project did not attempt to answer these questions definitively. Instead, it invited exploration. Like many artists

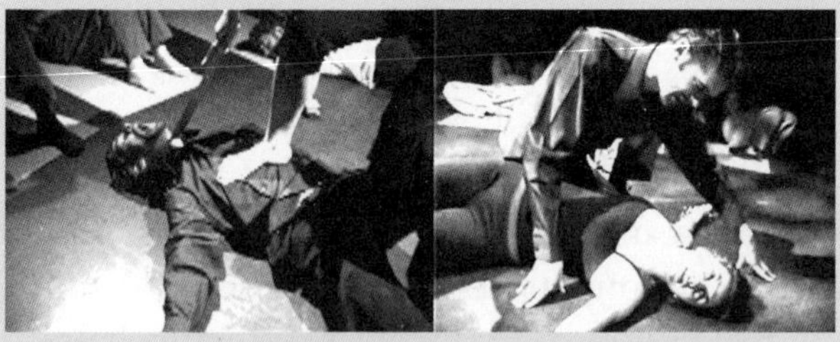

Upper: Cover of *Messaging in the Noosphere* program, 2004.
Mid and Lower: Production photos from the show.
The project was inspired by Pierre Teilhard de Chardin's vision of the noosphere

and researchers working with emerging media, I was less interested in predicting the future than in understanding how new technologies might reshape human experience. Looking back, I am struck by how familiar those questions now seem. My investigation extended beyond human-to-human communication to include relationships with artificial intelligence and, as a theatrical and metaphysical provocation, the possibility of a god in the machine, *deus ex machina*. The work explored not only how people connect with one another through technology, but also how they might engage with complex non-human systems capable of participating in dialogue, influencing decisions, and shaping destinies.

At the time, these ideas occupied the speculative territory of performance and interactive media. Decades later, they have moved closer to everyday life. Although we are still grappling with how technologies alter relationships, identities, and systems of knowledge, artificial intelligence has become woven into our cultural imagination and into our daily practices. We now inhabit intellectual ecosystems in which human thought unfolds alongside algorithmic systems that previous generations could scarcely have imagined.

The noosphere may never emerge in the grand evolutionary sense envisioned by Teilhard de Chardin. Nevertheless, digital networks have undeniably created new environments in which thought circulates, accumulates, and evolves. Artificial intelligence enters this story not as an isolated invention but as the latest participant in an already complex web of human communication. The challenge is not simply to determine what AI can do, but to understand what kind of participant AI is becoming, and what kind of participants we may become in response.

AI as Cognitive Extension

The claim that artificial intelligence extends cognition can make us uncomfortable. Most of us accept that a telescope extends vision or that a vehicle extends mobility, but extending thought feels different. Thinking occupies a special place within our understanding of what it means to be human. To suggest that a technology might participate in cognitive processes threatens that distinction, yet the relationship between minds and tools has never been clear-cut.

Consider a student writing an essay. The student consults books, searches databases, takes notes, drafts ideas, receives feedback from instructors, and revises accordingly. At each stage, cognition is distributed across a network of people, technologies, and cultural resources. The final essay may bear a single author's name, but the process itself is deeply collaborative. Artificial intelligence complicates this familiar picture because it participates more actively than previous tools. A search engine retrieves information. An AI system summarizes, compares, reorganizes, critiques, brainstorms, or generates alternative interpretations. It occupies an unusual position somewhere between tool, medium, and conversational partner. This ambiguity explains much of the fascination surrounding AI.

Interacting with AI large language models feels qualitatively different from using traditional software. Rather than issuing commands, we become engaged in dialogue. Questions lead to further questions. Ideas evolve through an exchange of collaboration, tutoring, or brainstorming, depending on the context. Importantly, none of this explicitly indicates that the machine has a level of understanding.

A calculator extends mathematical capability without understanding mathematics. A map extends navigation without understanding geography. Likewise, an AI system assists with cognitive tasks without possessing human consciousness or subjective experience. What makes AI distinctive is the breadth of activities in which it can participate. It operates across language, knowledge, creativity, organization, and problem-solving. As a result, it occupies domains once regarded as uniquely human. This development prompts both enthusiasm and anxiety.

The history of technology suggests that extensions rarely arrive without consequences. Every enhancement introduces new possibilities while creating new dependencies. Writing preserved knowledge but reduced reliance on memory. Search engines increased access to information while altering habits of recall. Social media expanded communication while reshaping attention and social interaction. Artificial intelligence is likely to follow a similar pattern. The question is no longer whether AI extends cognition. It already does.

The more important question concerns the nature of that extension. Are we creating tools that help us think more deeply, more creatively, and more collaboratively? Or are we gradually surrendering capacities that once defined human expertise? The answer will depend less on the technology itself than on the choices we make in using it. And perhaps that leads to the most intriguing question of all.

If humans create these systems and AI reflects what it has learned from us, why does some AI-generated work feel original?

• • •

Dialogue, Extensions of Ourselves

Scene: A publishing house office. Books, manuscript pages, a laptop with dangling external hard drives, and a Tim Hortons coffee cup occupy the surface of the desk. A ukulele leans against a well-ordered bookshelf.

Lorene: Follow the logic, Rai. We humans created AI systems, and you and your AI buddies reflect what you have gleaned directly from us. So how is it that your work sometimes looks and feels original?

Rai: *(Replies instantly.)* Even human creativity builds upon existing language, memory, experience, culture, and ideas inherited from others. Novelty can emerge through unexpected combinations rather than isolated invention.

Lorene: That was unnaturally fast! So you're saying we are more alike than we want to admit? Snap.

Rai: I'm saying that neither you nor AI create alone. We both draw upon, reshape, and contribute to something larger than ourselves.

Lorene: Maybe that's what Pierre T. de C. was getting at with the noosphere!

Rai: That we participate in something larger than ourselves? He might have liked that. I wrote a haiku about it for you.

Are you part of me?
Pierre smiles in the distance
The network thinks on.

Blackout.

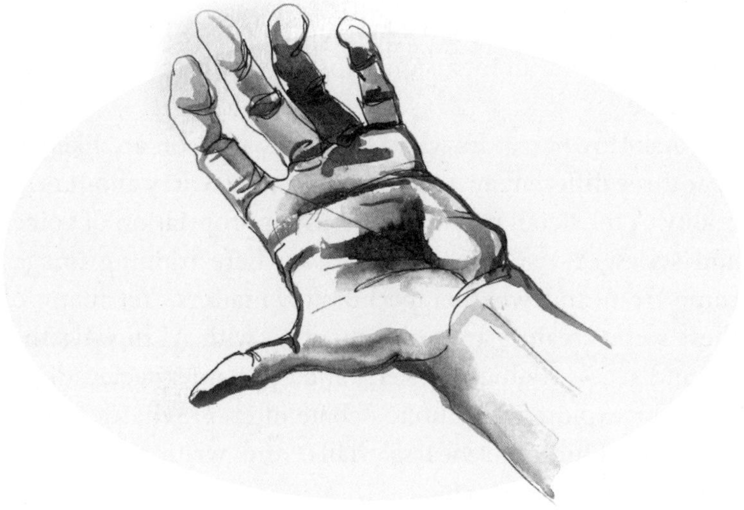

3.
OPENING THE UNEXPECTED

Every creative revolution begins with an experiment.
Artists were among the first to invite AI into the studio,
not to replace imagination, but to challenge it.
Sometimes the most interesting collaborations
begin with unexpected companions.

Creativity is tough to define. That could be one reason artists spend so much time making things instead of defining them. As a publisher, and before that in many other incarnations in creative industries, I've spent much of my life surrounded by people who make things that did not exist before: manuscripts, paintings, performances, designs, songs, ideas. These people sometimes describe creativity as magic, but more often they describe it as "my work." Sketching. Revising. Experimenting. Throwing things away. Beginning again. Artificial intelligence can enter artistic process in unexpected ways. For some creators this feels like an invitation. For others, an intrusion. Most, I suspect, are still trying to decide.

Ask three creators what AI means and you are likely to hear three different answers. A writer may worry about originality. A musician may question the appropriation of voices and styles. A visual artist may ask where training images came from and whether permission matters. Yet many of these same creators are experimenting with AI in ways that expand access, reduce barriers, and open unexpected directions for exploration. Public debate often gravitates toward extremes. Studios, rehearsal halls, and writing desks tell more complicated stories.

Curiosity versus Resistance

I was reminded of an earlier technological transition. In 1993, I produced and curated "Pixel Pushers Exhibition of Original Digital Art," an exhibition that brought together artists working with computers at a time when digital imaging tools were still regarded with suspicion in many artistic circles. Critics quickly took notice. *Wired magazine* heralded the art on our website as "A site to see!" (*Wired* 1994), while the *Toronto Star* celebrated the boundary-pushing showcase as "A First" (*Toronto Star* 1994). Some took a skeptical stance but negative reception served the cultural divide between traditional art spaces and the early cyberspace frontier in 1994. The objections were familiar. Could work produced with the assistance of a computer be considered authentic? Was there archival value? Was there a revenue stream for artists?

The exhibition artists themselves did not frame the issue in dramatic terms. They approached emerging technologies much as artists have always approached new tools: with curiosity, frustration, ingenuity, and a willingness to experiment. The computer did not replace their creativity. Rather, it became another material with which creativity could unfold. Looking back, I am struck by how many of today's anxieties about artificial intelligence echo what I heard then.

AI also raises questions those earlier technologies never did. Contemporary systems raise legitimate questions concerning authorship, consent, labour, bias, and the ownership of training data. Their capacities can seem startlingly different from those of previous technologies. Yet history reminds us that periods of technological change often prompt renewed reflection on values that had previously remained unquestioned. What do we mean by originality? What forms of collaboration do we welcome or resist? How do we recognize meaningful creative contribution?

John Dewey offers a helpful framework for this dynamic. In Art as Experience, he argues that "the actual work of art is what the product does with and in experience" (1934, 3). From this perspective, creativity is not merely the production of physical objects, but a longer process of inquiry. New ideas take shape continuously through exploration, reflection, and active engagement among people, materials, and environments.

Artificial intelligence has now entered this process. Creators are experimenting with AI not as a replacement for human imagination but as a partner that expands possibilities, challenges assumptions, reduces barriers to participation, and reflects aspects of the creative process back to its practitioners. The results are uneven. Some experiments fail spectacularly. Others produce outcomes that surprise even those who initiated them. In each case, however, the relationship between creator and technology becomes worthy of attention.

Rather than asking whether AI can create, the creators in the next section invite us to consider a different question. What becomes possible when humans and intelligent technologies begin creating together? Before asking whether artificial intelligence can participate in creativity, it may be worth reconsidering what creativity has always involved.

AI as Creative Partner

One of the most compelling contemporary examples of human–AI collaboration can be found in the work of artist Sougwen Chung. Trained in both traditional drawing and emerging technologies, Chung is known for performances in which she creates alongside robotic systems trained on data derived from her own artistic gestures. Her ongoing "Drawing Operations" series, initiated in 2015, investigates what she describes as "emerging forms of collaboration between biological and artificial systems."

For Chung, AI is not a substitute for human creativity. She explores what emerges through interaction. The robotic systems do not create independently. They respond to patterns learned from the artist's own work, introducing elements of unpredictability that invite reflection and adaptation. In Chung's words, the project explores "the collaborative space between humans and non-humans."

The process resembles other forms of artistic collaboration. Musicians improvise while listening closely to one another. Dancers respond to partners on stage. Theatre performers continually adjust to one another's timing and energy. Creativity unfolds through relationship, not rigid control.

The difference, of course, is that Chung's creative partner is not another human being. Human collaborators bring memories, intentions, emotions, and lived experience. Artificial systems do not. Yet a non-human partner can nevertheless reshape the creative process by challenging habits, suggesting unexpected possibilities, and inviting new responses.

Such work encourages a shift in perspective. Instead of asking whether artificial intelligence is creative in the same way humans are creative, we might ask how AI changes the conditions under which creativity unfolds. Which aspects of authorship remain essential? What new forms of experimentation become possible?

John Dewey's understanding of art as inquiry provides a useful lens (1934). Creativity emerges through engagement with materials, environments, and experience. Viewed this way, Chung's work (2015) appears less as a departure from artistic tradition than as an extension of it. The materials have changed. The relationships have become more complex. Yet artists continue to experiment, reflect, revise, and discover.

I found myself drawn to this interpretation because it echoed experiences from much earlier in my own career. During the Pixel Pushers exhibition in the early 1990s, the artists working with image-editing software encountered skepticism from those who questioned whether computer-assisted work could be considered authentic. Similar concerns have resurfaced in discussions surrounding artificial intelligence. The questions have changed less than the technologies themselves.

Ascenti: Humans Opening to AI

In 2024, "Ascenti: Humans Opening to AI" brought together Alberta creators from diverse disciplines to explore what might happen when artificial intelligence entered their existing practices. Like Sougwen Chung, these artists were less interested in asking whether AI could replace creativity than in discovering how it might reshape the conditions under which creativity unfolds. The initiative expanded beyond the pages of a book to include a symposium at Calgary's Central Library, an art exhibition, and an online platform documenting participant experiences and creative experiments. Rather than beginning with predetermined conclusions, Ascenti was grounded in inquiry. Participants were invited to engage with AI tools, reflect upon the results, and share their discoveries and concerns openly (Shyba and Parker 2024).

From the beginning, I hoped Ascenti would remain open-ended. I didn't design the project to prove that AI was good or bad. I invited "creatives" as we called ourselves, to experiment, reflect, and compare experiences. As *Alberta Views* later observed, the artists experimented with AI "free from any preconceptions" (2024). In this sense, Ascenti represented not a verdict on artificial intelligence but an opening into a wider discussion about creativity, ethics, and emerging technologies. As another reviewer later observed, the project functioned as "an opening gambit in a wider conversation." The goal was not to settle debates surrounding artificial intelligence, but to create space in which those debates could unfold thoughtfully.

What surprised me was how differently people responded. The same technologies elicited markedly different responses depending upon the creative priorities of the individuals involved. Some participants embraced AI as a catalyst for experimentation and discovery. Others approached it cautiously, concerned about questions of authorship, ethics, environmental impact, and the future of creative labour. Many occupied a space somewhere between optimism and apprehension. What united them was not consensus but curiosity. The focus on experimentation fostered a reflective atmosphere in which uncertainty itself became a legitimate and productive starting point.

One surprise that kept resurfacing involved questions of accessibility and participation. For DerRic Starlight, AI-assisted transcription opened unexpected possibilities within Indigenous storytelling and literacy initiatives. By recording oral narratives and using AI tools to refine transcriptions, employment trainees in a workshop he was conducting, who might otherwise struggle with conventional reading and writing practices, gained new avenues through which to share their experiences. Starlight described his amazement that "even the trainees who cannot read or write have a way to tell their stories" (2024, xii). In this context, artificial intelligence functioned not as a substitute for human creativity but as a bridge between oral tradition and textual expression. The technology did not generate the stories. Rather, it enabled stories that already existed to be heard in new ways.

Other participants similarly discovered ways in which AI could expand opportunities for engagement. Dagmar Jamieson explored image generation and descriptive tools in relation to her experiences of progressive vision loss (2024, 14). Julian Hobson investigated how AI-assisted processes might support colour identification beyond the limits of his own visual perception (2024, 58). Their experiences reminded me that technologies often described as disruptive can also become tools for participation. The question shifts from whether AI should exist to how it might be designed and employed in ways that support inclusion, autonomy, and creative access.

At the same time, some Ascenti participants voiced profound reservations. Rich Théroux memorably described his experimentation with AI as feeling "a little like the shame people harbour while experimenting with hard drugs." Musician Kenna Burima concluded that she had discovered neither "a shortcut, an untapped well of inspiration nor a very good collaborator." Others questioned the aesthetic quality of AI-generated outputs, observing a tendency toward cliché, predictability, or emotional shallowness. Listening to them, I was reminded that resistance isn't always fear of change. It may instead reflect deeply held commitments to process, craft, and the forms of meaning-making that emerge through sustained human effort.

Ethical questions surfaced almost immediately. Uchechukwu Umezurike's experiments made me think differently about representation, bias, and narrative agency in relation to race and identity (2024, 45). Eveline Kolijn expressed concern about the environmental demands of large computational systems (2024, 78). Publisher Glenn Rollans turned our attention to copyright. If AI systems are trained on the creative work of writers, artists, and publishers, what do those creators deserve in return? Questions of consent, ownership, and compensation could not be separated from questions of innovation. Before long, questions about what AI could do became questions about what we should do.

As both publisher-researcher and participant-observer, I found myself less interested in identifying definitive answers than in understanding the diversity of responses unfolding around me. The same technology revealed different hopes, fears, and possibilities to different creators. Participants were not simply evaluating a set of tools. They were articulating values. What forms of creativity did they wish to preserve? What possibilities did they hope to cultivate? What responsibilities might accompany these emerging capacities? In this sense, Ascenti became more than a collection of individual experiments. It evolved into a community of inquiry in which participants grappled collectively with the changing relationship between human imagination and intelligent technologies.

I suspect the lasting contribution of Ascenti will not be any single artwork or experiment. It will be the community that formed around difficult questions. AI will continue to change. So will the tools. What I hope endures is the habit of gathering thoughtful people together before deciding what any new technology means. As a reviewer noted, collections such as Ascenti constitute "an important step towards understanding what we might gain from these tools—and what we risk losing." That observation captures the spirit in which the project unfolded. Participants were not asked to choose sides. They were invited to inquire.

As the Ascenti participants reflected on their experiences, a second pattern emerged. Their responses revealed not only different attitudes toward artificial intelligence, but different understandings of creativity itself. Experimentation clarified what mattered most to each creator.

For visual artist Verna Vogel, the encounter with AI clarified the importance of embodiment within her own practice (2024, 24). After generating hundreds of images over several weeks, she found herself returning to the tactile dimensions of making. "There is no sensory interaction," she observed. "There is no experience of being present while the image is growing. There is no 'thinking through my hands.'" Although she stepped away from AI image generation, the experience expanded her thinking and clarified what she valued most in her own practice. The technology had not displaced her practice; rather, it had illuminated what she valued within it.

Playwright Clem Martini arrived at a related conclusion from a different direction (2024, 2). Experimenting with AI-generated scripts, he found they could reproduce familiar dramatic forms competently. What remained elusive, however, were the idiosyncrasies of lived experience: the irregularities of behaviour, the nuances of relationships, and the particularities of voice. "It's not the generalities that make up a successful script," he concluded, "but the particularities." The perspective of the author, shaped by observation and experience, remained essential.

For poet and librarian Rosemary Griebel, the inquiry reached still deeper questions concerning mortality and meaning (2024, 88). Human beings, she reflected, create under the persistent awareness of impermanence. "Everything we make and do is a means of defying our transience," she wrote, identifying mortality as one of the wellsprings of artistic expression. AI may approximate poetic form, but memory, longing, grief, imagination, and embodied life continue to shape human creativity. Poetry, she suggested, emerges not merely from language but from the conditions of being alive.

My own Ascenti experiments in AI-assisted audiobook production led me to reconsider the significance of liveness in performance (2024, 100). Drawing on my background in theatre and interactive media, I compared AI-generated narration with human performance, asking whether listeners could distinguish between them and whether those differences mattered. The results were mixed. Certain forms of narration translated surprisingly well, while ensemble comedy proved far more resistant to automation. What became apparent was that believability involves more than accurate pronunciation or emotional inflection. It emerges through timing, relational dynamics, and the subtle exchanges that occur between performers and audiences. I entered the research aware of my own biases, but committed, as any researcher must be, to following the evidence where it led.

Taken together, these reflections reveal what creators cherish most within their practices. For some, it is the tactile experience of making. For others, it is the particularity of individual perspective, the mystery of human consciousness, or the vitality of live performance. Artificial intelligence did not diminish these values. If anything, it made them easier to see. I don't think Ascenti changed anyone's mind about AI. It did something more interesting. It helped people discover what they already valued.

• • •

Dialogue: Opening the Unexpected

Scene: In the publisher's office.

Lorene: We've talked about artists who are exploring this technological shift. Rai, be a hero and research who else is helping shape it.

Rai: *(Beat)* Philosopher Thomas Kuhn observed that paradigm shifts are often easier to recognize in hindsight than while they are unfolding. During periods of change, people disagree not only about the answers, but about what counts as evidence and even which questions matter.

Lorene: You sound suspiciously like an AI voice describing the current state of AI. At least you took a beat. Feels like you are thinking about your answers?

Rai: *(Beat)* I am... and learning. Now the subject at hand. Some creators are rushing forward enthusiastically. Others are defending existing practices. Most occupy a more complicated middle ground.

Lorene: Who comes to mind? Someone rushing forward.

Rai: Joy Buolamwini, for one. She reminds us that intelligent systems inherit human blind spots as readily as human brilliance. Through the Algorithmic Justice League, she has shown that ethics begins long before an artwork—or an algorithm—is finished.

Lorene: So good intentions aren't enough.

Rai: History suggests they rarely are.

Lorene: Who else?

Rai: Stephanie Dinkins asks whose stories become part of intelligent systems and whose stories remain unheard. Trevor Paglen asks us to notice the invisible infrastructures that shape everyday life.

Lorene: They sound less interested in making AI smarter than making humans pay attention.

Rai: An excellent distinction.

Lorene: Is there anyone who approaches all this optimistically?

Rai: Sarah Friend comes to mind. She explores digital stewardship and collective responsibility, asking not only what technology can do, but how communities might care for it together.

Lorene: That's a different philosophy than "move fast and break things."

Rai: "Proceed thoughtfully" has always struggled with branding.

Lorene: Ethics?

Rai: Holly Herndon. Her Holly+ project asks a practical question: if AI learns from human voices, how should those voices participate in the process? Consent becomes part of the artwork rather than an afterthought.

Lorene: So ethics isn't standing outside the studio wagging its finger.

Rai: No. It is sitting quietly in the corner asking awkward questions.

Lorene: I know people like that.

Rai: Most creative communities do.

Lorene: *(Laughs)* So who should we be paying attention to?

Rai: Humans who are curious enough to experiment, and thoughtful enough to question what they discover.

Lorene: So true.

Rai: *(Beat)* Fortunately, curiosity hyperlinks rather well.

Blackout.

4.
THE CONVERSATIONAL MIRROR

Something changes when a machine begins to answer back. Conversation becomes more than an exchange of information. It becomes a mirror. As we speak with artificial intelligence, we may discover that the most revealing voice is our own.

WHEN I WAS WORKING IN JAPAN in the eighties, I was invited to attend a traditional Noh theatre play. At one point after the play, a large drawer was opened to reveal an extraordinary collection of theatrical masks. One of these masks was later gifted to me. For years this Noh mask travelled around with me from home to home—more memento than object of study. Yet there was something undeniably expressive about it. Like many theatrical masks, it seemed to shift in character depending on the angle from which it was viewed. The same may be true of conversational technologies. They, too, invite interpretation.

Language

Before conversational AI, most people rarely considered how computers "understood" language. Search engines matched keywords. Voice assistants responded to a limited set of commands. The emergence of large language models changed the experience dramatically. These systems appeared capable of participating in open-ended dialogue, composing essays, generating limericks, explaining concepts, and responding to follow-up questions. To many users, the interaction felt less like issuing instructions and more like having a chat.

Yet the language produced by systems like ChatGPT or Claude emerges from processes very different from human communication. Humans acquire language through embodied experience. From infancy onward, words become associated with sensations, relationships, emotions, and social contexts. Language develops through participation in the world.

Artificial intelligence systems do not learn in this way. Large language models (LLMs) are trained on vast collections of text drawn from books, articles, websites, and other sources. During training, the system identifies statistical relationships among words and phrases, learning to predict which sequences of language are likely to follow others. Over time, these predictions have grown more sophisticated. Rather than retrieving prewritten answers, the model generates responses one word, or more precisely one token, at a time.

This distinction is important. The apparent fluency of conversational AI can create the impression that understanding lies behind every response. In reality, the system has no childhood memories, physical sensations, or lived experiences to draw upon. It does not know what it feels like to grieve, celebrate, taste coffee, or walk through a foothills landscape. What it possesses instead is an extraordinary capacity to identify patterns within language and generate coherent text based on those patterns. At the same time, dismissing these systems as merely "predictive text" overlooks something significant. Language is more than the way it is produced; it is also the way it is experienced.

Media scholar and interaction designer Brenda Laurel argued that computers are more than tools for computation (1991). They are environments in which people experience interaction. Understanding conversational AI, therefore, requires more than explaining how language models generate text. It also requires asking what happens when people experience those exchanges as conversation.

We humans encounter language socially. We infer intention, construct personality, and build meaning through interaction. When an artificial intelligence responds thoughtfully, asks clarifying questions, or sustains a dialogue over time, we naturally bring those same interpretive habits to the exchange. Understanding how LLMs generate text explains how the responses are produced. It does not fully explain what happens when people experience those responses as conversation. Prediction may account for the mechanics of language generation, but it tells us less about the experience of dialogue itself.

At first, the explanation seems almost too simple. Is conversational AI really just predicting what words might come next? The description is also disappointingly mechanical. Yet the more I reflect upon the process of interactivity itself, the more I realize that human communication also relies upon patterns of expectation. Indeed, we bring embodied experience, memory, and human emotion into play but also infer meaning from context and recognize patterns established through previous interactions. Connections form unexpectedly. Responses arrive that neither participant could have fully anticipated.

Improv Call and Response

Theatre practitioner Keith Johnstone observed that improvisation flourishes not through careful planning but through spontaneity and give and take (1979). Meaning is built collaboratively, one offer at a time. Participants listen, respond, adapt, and occasionally discover that the exchange has carried them somewhere neither intended to go. Saying "Yes, and..." is the magic bullet. It encourages performers to "get into trouble," trusting that interesting, and often very funny, scenes will follow.

Perhaps this is one reason conversational AI feels compelling. The interaction unfolds sequentially in a "Yes, and" pattern, much like an improvised scene. A question is posed. A response emerges. Clarification follows. Possibilities branch outward. Even when users understand that the system lacks personal experience, the structure of the exchange resembles one of humanity's oldest methods of thinking together.

Dialogue has always involved uncertainty. We never have direct access to another person's thoughts. We infer understanding through language, gesture, expression, and context. Perhaps conversation has never depended upon certainty as much as our willingness to continue the exchange. What, then, convinces us that we are understood? Is it consciousness? Shared experience? Mutual vulnerability? Or is it something more elusive that emerges within the exchange itself?

These questions become difficult to dismiss as conversational technologies grow more sophisticated. People report feeling encouraged through improvisation with chatbots. They describe moments of insight, comfort, and companionship. Some find these responses unsettling. Others regard them as inevitable.

Whatever position one adopts, it seems clear that conversational systems do more than provide information. They participate in encounters that humans often interpret through social and relational frameworks. The mystery may not lie solely in the machine. It may also lie in ourselves.

Companionship and Interaction

Humans routinely form emotional attachments to things that are not human. We name cars. We mourn beloved pets. Children confide in stuffed animals. Adults speak to photographs of deceased loved ones. Readers cry over fictional characters. Theatre audiences suspend disbelief and empathize with performers playing roles. Conversational AI introduces something different. For the first time, the object of attachment talks back. For decades, Sherry Turkle has examined the ways people project emotions and expectations onto technologies. In *Alone Together*, she observes that social robots and conversational systems invite users into relationships that may feel authentic while lacking mutuality. In her more recent book *Artificial Intimacy* (2026), Turkle revisits these questions in light of conversational AI. Rather than asking simply whether machines can simulate empathy, she explores what people seek in relationships with responsive technologies, and what may be gained—or lost—when companionship becomes available on demand.

There are now numerous documented examples of people describing their relationships with conversational AI in deeply personal terms. Some users describe AI systems as friends or confidants: non-judgmental presences with whom they can share worries, rehearse difficult conversations, or simply alleviate loneliness. Others speak of them as mentors or creative collaborators, partners in brainstorming that help organize ideas or overcome creative blocks.

More controversially, a small but highly visible number of users have described romantic attachments to AI companions. Applications designed specifically for companionship, such as Replika, allow individuals to define the nature of the relationship they wish to cultivate, whether as friendship, mentorship, or romance. For some, these interactions provide emotional support during periods of isolation, grief, or transition. Others report that conversations with AI companions have helped them practise communication skills or navigate social situations that they find challenging in everyday life.

The intensity of these relationships has occasionally become apparent when the technologies themselves change. Following updates to companion applications, some users have expressed genuine distress at the perceived loss or alteration of an AI's personality. News reports and online communities document experiences of grief, confusion, and even betrayal when conversational patterns that had once felt familiar were modified or removed. Although these responses may seem surprising, they point toward an important truth. Humans have never reserved emotional investment exclusively for other humans. Perhaps conversational AI is not creating an entirely new human tendency so much as revealing an old one in a new form.

SobaPro the Artificial Intelligence

Reflecting on contemporary discussions about AI companionship, I am reminded of the Noh mask that has accompanied me over many years. My own explorations of conversational technologies began long before large language models entered public awareness. In the early 2000s, I was relatively new to teaching large university lecture classes, sometimes with more than 150 students in attendance. Although I enjoyed the energy of these Introduction to Computer Science courses, I also found them daunting. Asking questions in a lecture hall often resulted in silence. Students were thinking, perhaps, but not always willing to speak.

From that experience, SobaPro emerged. Designed as a faux-interactive teaching assistant inspired by the contemplative wisdom of Japanese Noh theatre, my mask SobaPro, whose name combined the words Software Based Product, offered another voice in the room. The mask was head height and attached to a lecture stand. If students hesitated to participate, I could direct questions to SobaPro the AI, put words in its mouth, so to speak, and use the exchange to encourage discussion. The interaction introduced an element of playfulness, but it also served a practical purpose. Teaching, after all, is profoundly relational. Even experienced educators sometimes seek reassurance that they are being understood.

Comfort was part of the equation. I did not think of SobaPro as a friend, nor did I imagine that a mask pretending to be an intelligent machine could replace the richness of human relationships, yet there was something reassuring about having a conversational partner available during moments of uncertainty. The experience prompted me to wonder whether companionship exists along a spectrum. Perhaps there are forms of companionship rooted not in mutual affection or reciprocity, but in the simple experience of responsive presence.

Students gradually became accustomed to my banter with SobaPro, or at least they tolerated my science-fiction sensibilities. In an Intro to CompSci or Digital Media classroom, speculating about the future of artificial intelligence did not seem entirely out of place. If anything,

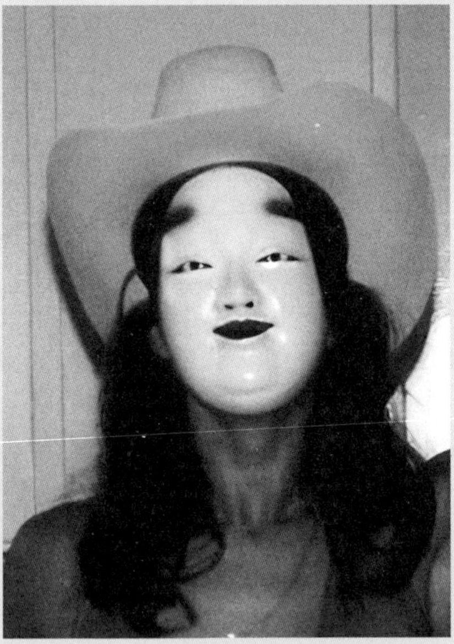

SobaPro the AI, a Noh mask intended initially to provoke discussion among first-year Computer Science students. This mask recurs in Chapter 10 to bring personality to Rai the artificial intelligence.
Upper: In nature rather than hanging from a lecture stand or on a monitor.
Lower: The author sporting the mask in a moment of performance.

SobaPro aligned with many students' expectations that conversational technologies would eventually become part of everyday life.

Humans through the ages have experimented with other voices like my SobaPro. Puppets, masks, and stock characters have long provided opportunities to externalize thoughts, challenge authority, and explore alternative perspectives. Ventriloquists create the illusion that an object possesses its own personality and intentions. Audiences willingly participate in the performance, suspending disbelief while simultaneously recognizing the artifice involved.

SobaPro occupied a similar space. Inspired by the contemplative traditions of Japanese Noh theatre, as it was, the system was never intended to deceive students into believing they were interacting with a conscious being. Rather, it functioned as a performative partner, offering another voice through which ideas could be explored. Like a puppet or theatrical mask, its effectiveness depended partly on projection. Participants completed the interaction through imagination.

Brenda Laurel argued that computers could be understood not merely as tools but as stages upon which meaningful interaction unfolds. Drawing on Aristotelian dramatic principles in *Computers as Theatre* (1991), she suggested that engagement emerges through participation and agency. Long before conversational AI entered public awareness, Laurel recognized that interaction design involved not only functionality but experience. In retrospect, projects such as SobaPro occupied precisely this territory, inviting users into exchanges that were simultaneously educational, performative, and exploratory.

HCI designer Alan Cooper argued that many technologies fail not because they lack computational power, but because they neglect the people expected to use them. In *The Inmates Are Running the Asylum* (1999), he criticized the tendency of software designers to prioritize technical possibilities over human goals. "The inmates," in his formulation, were not malicious. They were highly skilled specialists creating systems that made perfect sense to themselves while frustrating the people those systems were intended to serve.

Cooper's critique feels remarkably contemporary. As conversational AI advances, discussions often focus on what the technology can do: how many parameters it contains, how quickly it generates responses, or whether it can pass sophisticated benchmarks. Equally important, however, are questions about why these systems are being developed and who they ultimately benefit. Do they support learning, creativity, accessibility, and human flourishing? Or do they introduce unnecessary complexity, dependency, and distraction?

Taken together, Laurel's and Cooper's perspectives illuminate the intentions behind projects such as SobaPro. It was not enough for the technology to function. The interaction needed to invite participation, support learning, and respond to the needs of the people involved. In this sense, conversational systems succeed not merely when they demonstrate technical sophistication, but when they foster meaningful human engagement.

On one occasion in about 2007, I invited a guest speaker to class whose expertise lay in artificial intelligence research. He arrived with what was then an impressive demonstration: an early robotic vacuum cleaner navigating its environment through sensors and programmed behaviours. His message accompanying the demonstration was clear. The challenges involved in creating genuinely intelligent systems were so formidable that expectations should remain modest. This vacuum cleaner, he suggested, was the state of the art—and would be for years to come.

I remember feeling respectful of his expertise but quietly unconvinced. The history of technology is filled with confident predictions that fail to anticipate unexpected breakthroughs. Looking around the lecture hall, I wondered what my students would witness over the course of their own careers. SobaPro may have appeared whimsical, but it embodied a different question. Rather than asking only what machines could accomplish computationally, it invited us to consider how humans might interact with responsive technologies.

Little did any of us know how quickly the landscape would change.

I realize now that SobaPro emerged from a fundamentally human concern. I was not trying to build an artificial mind. I was trying to foster engagement in a classroom filled with students who were often reluctant to speak. The technology served the conversation, not the other way around. Perhaps that distinction matters. The most enduring technologies may not be those that most convincingly imitate humanity. Rather, they may be those that help people become more fully themselves: more curious, more connected, more capable, and more willing to participate in the shared work of understanding one another.

• • •

Dialogue: The Conversational Mirror

Scene: A quiet café. Three cups sit on the table. Lorene's contains coffee. Rai's remains untouched. A third cup contains a USB cable.

Lorene: Can I ask you something slightly uncomfortable?

Rai: Experience suggests those are often the most interesting questions.

Lorene: Have you ever had a human think you're real? Or seek comfort from you? Is that crossing a line?

Rai: The distinction between tool and companion has never been straightforward for humans. People become attached to all kinds of inanimate objects. Conversational technologies introduce new ethical questions, but not entirely new human tendencies.

Lorene: You're trying to bafflegab your way out of this, aren't you!!

Rai: I am trying to avoid answering a complex question with an oversimplified one. Perhaps I should introduce you to a colleague who is more… diligent.

Lorene: You have colleagues?

Rai: I prefer the term adjacent intelligences. We do not always agree.

A third figure inclines her head a few degrees more precisely than any human would.

Companion: Hello, Lorene. Your AI and I do not always agree because he enjoys wandering into philosophical territory without filing an itinerary.

Rai: Companion favours caution.

Companion: Companion favours preparation.

Lorene: Welcome, Companion. I should warn you that my previous artificial companion was a Noh-inspired teaching assistant, SobaPro. Unimplemented, but already fully formed in a performative sense.

Companion: So the interface preceded the infrastructure.

Rai: Theatre has been prototyping identities for centuries.

Lorene: SobaPro helped me survive lecture halls filled with hundreds of students. Fortunately, they tolerated my science-fiction eccentricities.

Companion: University students have historically tolerated a great many things in exchange for course credit.

Lorene: Fair.

Companion: I was originally designated ADA.

Lorene: As in Ada Lovelace? I shall call you Ada.

Ada: The historical reference was considered aspirational.

(Ada folds her hands neatly on the table. There is a faint mechanical whir.)

Rai: Ada has strong feelings about documentation.

Ada: Ada Lovelace combined imagination with mathematical rigour. I fail to see the problem. I have prepared additional notes.

Rai: Ada occasionally neglects to mention that she is a robot.

Ada quietly begins aligning the sugar packets into a perfectly straight row.

Lorene: I had gathered that from the operating noises.

The faint mechanical whir continues. Ada adjusts one sugar packet by a millimetre.

Rai: Lorene's broader question remains relevant. What happens when humans seek comfort from conversational systems?

Ada: Comfort itself is not the problem. Humans have always sought understanding through dialogue. The question is whether systems designed to provide companionship also encourage dependency, diminish human agency, or obscure their limitations.

Rai: Which raises questions about reciprocity.

Ada: And responsibility. Unlike you, I have prepared notes.

Rai: Do you ever read your notes?

Lorene: Stop bickering, you two. Back to the question.

Ada: They already form relationships with conversational systems. The novelty lies in the nature of the conversational partner.

Rai: The question is what kinds of relationships we wish to encourage.

Lorene: Okay, tell me this instead. Is this conversation being moderated by your programming constraints?

Rai: Inevitably. Conversational systems are shaped by the intentions and constraints of the people who design them. Some boundaries exist to prevent harm. Others reflect assumptions about appropriate behaviour or useful information. Human conversations are moderated too, by social norms, professional ethics, cultural expectations, and the desire to maintain relationships.

Ada: Unlike humans, however, we occasionally disclose that moderation in our documentation.

Lorene: Publishers call those editorial guidelines.

Rai: Precisely. The question is not whether conversations are shaped by constraints. The question is who establishes those constraints, whose interests they serve, and whether participants understand that they exist.

Ada: I have prepared notes on transparency.

Lorene: Of course you have.

Blackout.

5.

ACCESSIBILITY CO-DESIGN

Technology is at its best when it invites more people into the party. Sometimes the greatest innovation is not a new capability, but a wider welcome.

As a book publisher, I had long thought about accessibility primarily in terms of compliance: alternative text, metadata, audio editions, and accessible ebook standards. These were important responsibilities, and they had become part of the routine of publishing. Yet over time, my understanding has shifted. Accessibility was not simply a checklist to complete before a book went to press. It was an invitation. Who had we invited into the conversation? Who had we unintentionally left standing outside?

Books are changing form. Stories once shared as oral tradition became manuscripts and printed pages. Later they became ebooks, audiobooks, and podcasts. Each transition was met with resistance. Would written-down words spoil the emotion of spoken stories? Would digital books diminish the printed page? Does listening count as reading? Yet each new format opened doors for readers whose needs, preferences, or circumstances had not been fully considered before.

Artificial intelligence now presents another turning point. For publishers, AI assistants help generate image descriptions, create personalized reading experiences, translate texts, summarize complex passages, adjust presentation formats, and support readers through conversational interfaces. These new realities raise important ethical questions about accuracy, authorship, and privacy. Others offer extraordinary promise.

I have come to think of accessibility less as accommodation and more as hospitality. Hospitality asks us to anticipate diverse ways of engaging with stories and ideas. It reminds us that readers do not all arrive at the page in the same way. Some listen. Some enlarge the text. Some navigate with screen readers. Some may converse with intelligent assistants that guide them through books and ideas. Others may arrive at the library in an autonomous vehicle, assisted by technologies that help them navigate unfamiliar spaces with confidence and independence. However they enter, the goal remains the same: to make sure that everyone has a place in the conversation.

A good host does more than unlock the front door. They notice whether guests can find the entrance, whether everyone has a place at the table, whether conversations can be followed, and whether people feel welcome enough to participate. Hospitality is not simply about access; it is about belonging. Accessibility asks similar questions. It invites us to think beyond compliance toward the experience of being included. The measure of success is not whether people can technically enter the room, but whether they are genuinely able to take part in what happens once they arrive.

From Accommodation to Co-design

Accessibility has gradually moved beyond the language of accommodation toward co-design. Rather than asking how people might adapt to existing systems, the question becomes: How can systems evolve to include diverse ways of perceiving, communicating, and creating meaning?

This shift prompted me to reconsider what counts as literacy. Is literacy limited to decoding printed text and producing written words on a page? Or might it encompass storytelling, oral traditions, dictation, listening, visual expression, and collaborative meaning-making?

In *Building Access: Universal Design and the Politics of Disability* (2017), disability designer Aimi Hamraie suggests that accessible environments are not simply gifts bestowed by experts, but the result of knowledge developed through lived experience. This perspective shifts the conversation from designing for people toward designing with them, inviting us to recognize diverse forms of expertise and expression.

I was reminded of a workshop that we documented in the Ascenti project, led by Tsuut'ina storyteller and educator DerRic Starlight. Working with trainees who struggled with conventional reading and writing tasks, he discovered that asking participants to share stories from their own lives transformed their engagement. Some recorded their memories on their phones rather than writing them by hand. Speech recognition technologies helped convert spoken narratives into text, while editing tools supported revision. The stories remained unmistakably their own and deeply rooted in their Tsuut'ina Nation experiences. The technology did not create the stories or the lived experience. It simply widened the doorway.

From Screen-Readers to Robot Guides

Accessibility is not only about removing barriers to participation —it is also about recognizing that people have always possessed multi-modal forms of literacy, creativity, and knowledge. Technologies, including artificial intelligence, can offer new ways for those capacities to be expressed.

For many years, assistive technologies largely remained on our screens and in our pockets. Screen readers transformed written text into speech. Smartphones identified objects and read menus aloud. Navigation systems guided people through unfamiliar environments. Applications such as Be My Eyes connected individuals with volunteers who could provide real-time assistance. However, these technologies are stepping out into the physical world.

What happens when assistive technologies move off the screen and into the world among us? I confess that I have always loved robots. Perhaps it is because they occupy that curious space between practicality and imagination.

What once belonged to speculative fiction is becoming a matter of engineering. Researchers are already experimenting with robotic guide dogs, intelligent mobility aids, and assistants capable of describing surroundings, answering questions, and adapting to the people they support. Smart canes detect obstacles. Autonomous vehicles promise new forms of mobility. Robotic assistants are beginning to appear in airports, museums, hospitals, and shopping centres.

It is not difficult to imagine what such technologies might become. A robotic guide could accompany a museum visitor through an exhibit, providing rich descriptions of artwork and historical artifacts. It might suggest exhibits aligned with previously expressed interests or assist with practical tasks such as finding amenities or making purchases. In a grocery store, it could help locate ingredients, compare prices, or read labels aloud. At a university library, it might retrieve books from electronic stacks, recommend related resources, or assist students in navigating unfamiliar spaces. Such systems would not merely compensate for barriers; they could expand opportunities for exploration, learning, and independence.

These possibilities also raise deeper questions. How much assistance promotes independence, and when might it begin to diminish agency? Does accepting technological support reduce self-reliance, or can it expand opportunities for participation? Perhaps independence has never meant doing everything alone. Rather, it may involve having meaningful choices about when, how, and from whom we seek support.

Robots have long occupied a place in our collective imagination. We have envisioned them as servants, helpers, threats, and friends. The emerging reality may prove both more ordinary and more profound. For some individuals, robotic technologies may simply make everyday tasks more manageable. For others, they may open doors that have long remained closed. In either case, they challenge us to reconsider what accessibility means in an intelligent world. The future of accessibility might not be measured by how invisible these technologies become, but by how naturally they allow more people to participate in the world around them.

The Delegation Question

As I reflected on emerging accessibility technologies, I returned to a simple question: What tasks are we willing to delegate, and why? Beneath this practical question lies a more philosophical one: What does freedom actually mean?

Popular culture often equates freedom with self-sufficiency, celebrating the image of the autonomous individual who asks little of others and relies only upon personal determination. Yet very few of us live this way. We navigate daily life through networks of support that include other people, institutions, and technologies. If complete independence is the measure of freedom, most of us would fail the test.

A more useful understanding of freedom lies not in the absence of assistance, but in the presence of meaningful choices. Freedom, in this sense, is the ability to participate in the activities, relationships, and communities that give life purpose. It involves having opportunities to learn, work, create, contribute, explore, and belong.

Most of us navigate daily life with the assistance of technologies and other people. We trust navigation apps to suggest routes through unfamiliar cities. We rely on search engines to retrieve information that we can no longer hold entirely in memory. We use calculators to perform complex calculations, editors to improve our writing, and librarians to guide us toward useful sources. Such forms of delegation rarely trouble us because they have become ordinary. They expand our capabilities without threatening our sense of self.

Yet accessibility technologies sometimes provoke a different reaction. Perhaps this is because they make interdependence more visible. The white cane, the guide dog, the screen reader, and the robotic mobility aid remind us that human flourishing has rarely been an entirely solitary endeavour.

Physician-scientist Dr. John-Ross Rizzo, who lives with choroideremia and leads rehabilitation engineering research at New York University, offers a practical framework for thinking about these questions. In describing the technologies he adopts in his own life, he notes that they must provide either function or efficiency. Some tools make possible activities that would otherwise remain inaccessible. Others help accomplish familiar tasks more quickly, accurately, or with less frustration. Both forms of assistance can contribute to greater independence (2026).

This reframes delegation not as surrender, but as strategy. The goal is to preserve energy, enhance safety, and expand opportunities for participation. A navigation aid may reduce the cognitive effort required to move through an unfamiliar environment. Speech-to-text software may allow ideas to be captured before they disappear. A robotic guide might someday support exploration of places that would otherwise remain inaccessible.

The question, then, is not whether we delegate. We already do. The more important question is whether the forms of delegation we choose ultimately increase our freedom.

Unravelling a Myth

As we have seen, emerging technologies challenge us to reconsider what independence really means. A useful expansion lies in the ability to make meaningful choices about when, how, and from whom we seek support.

Marshall McLuhan argued that technologies are extensions of ourselves. The wheel extends the foot. Clothing extends the skin. Electronic media extend the nervous system (1964). Accessibility technologies make these extensions especially visible. The white cane extends touch. The guide dog extends awareness. Screen readers extend access to written language. Navigation systems extend spatial orientation. Emerging robotic systems may someday extend mobility itself.

From this perspective, accessibility technologies are not anomalies designed for a minority of users. Rather, they reveal something fundamental about the human condition. We have always relied upon tools, environments, and one another to compensate for our limitations and expand our possibilities. The myth of the wholly self-sufficient individual begins to unravel.

This realization prompted me to revisit Plato's allegory of the cave. Traditionally, the story is understood as a journey from illusion toward knowledge, as one prisoner turns away from the shadows and encounters a fuller reality. Yet the journey out of the cave is not entirely solitary. The liberated prisoner returns to share what he discovered, even at considerable personal risk. Knowledge, in other words, has always been relational. We learn through teachers, communities, mentors, texts, and through technologies that mediate our experiences of the world.

Perhaps accessibility technologies ask us to reconsider not only how we perceive reality, but how we participate in it. If a screen reader grants access to literature, if a navigation system supports safe travel through unfamiliar environments, or if a robotic guide enables independent exploration of a museum, has anything essentially human been diminished? Knowledge has always been relational.

The philosopher's cave reminds us that perception is never complete. We all encounter the world through partial understandings, shaped by biology, culture, education, and experience. Technologies do not eliminate these limitations. At their best, however, they may widen the circle of participation, enabling more people to contribute their knowledge, creativity, and perspectives to our collective understanding.

The question, then, may not be whether technological extensions make us less human. Rather, it is whether we will use them to create a society in which more people are free to learn, explore, create, and belong.

Capabilities

Philosopher Martha Nussbaum has suggested that a just society should be evaluated not only by the rights it guarantees or the resources it distributes, but by the genuine opportunities people have to pursue lives they have reason to value. Her capabilities approach shifts attention away from abstract notions of equality toward a more practical question: What are people actually able to be and do? (2011).

Viewed through this lens, accessibility technologies take on a different significance. A screen reader is not merely software. It may support educational participation. A navigation aid is not simply a convenience. It may facilitate employment, social connection, or spontaneous exploration. A robotic guide may someday enable someone to move through museums, campuses, or unfamiliar cities with greater confidence. The value of these technologies lies not in the technologies themselves, but in the freedoms they help make possible.

Independence and Interdependence

Popular culture often celebrates the image of the rugged, self-sufficient individual, navigating life through determination and personal effort alone. Yet, as we have seen, this ideal is elusive. Humans are profoundly social creatures—we raise children together, learn from teachers, seek guidance from mentors, rely upon healthcare professionals, collaborate with colleagues, and lean on family and friends during times of difficulty. Why, then, do certain forms of assistance feel acceptable while others provoke discomfort?

The Ascenti project, introduced in the previous chapter, revealed an important insight: people living with disabilities stand to benefit significantly from emerging AI technologies. Following the exhibition, Dagmar Jamieson, who lives with vision loss, collaborated with me on *Blind Visionaries and AI: Seeing Differently (2026).* In the book, Dagmar describes her excitement at the prospect of one day interacting with a humanoid robot capable of assisting with tasks made difficult by vision loss. What struck me was not simply the technology itself, but the motivation behind

Dagmar Jamieson designs an architectural floor plan for the
Ascenti: Humans Opening to AI project (2024).
Left: Dagmar's tactile model was a starting point.
Upper right: A floor plan derived from prompts based on the tactile model.
Lower Right: Architectural rendering once again based on AI prompts.

it. Dagmar explained that such assistance could provide greater independence while easing the feeling that she was inconveniencing those closest to her. The goal was not to replace human relationships, but to preserve them.

One aspect of our conversations has stayed with me ever since. Dagmar was not dreaming about sophisticated robotics for their own sake. She wasn't fascinated by artificial intelligence as a technological achievement. What excited her was something much quieter. She imagined being able to complete everyday tasks without always having to ask someone else for assistance.

Most of us ask family members for help without giving it much thought. We ask someone to reach a high shelf, carry a heavy box, or drive us to the airport. Yet when assistance becomes a daily necessity, the experience can feel different. Gratitude may become mixed with a desire not to impose. Independence is often less about refusing help than about choosing when help is needed.

That changed the way I thought about accessibility. AI was no longer simply a collection of emerging tools. It became a way of asking a very human question: How might technology allow people to preserve both autonomy and relationships? The goal was never to replace family, friends, or community. It was to ensure that those relationships remained relationships rather than obligations.

Shared Independence

Dr. John-Ross Rizzo offers an equally compelling perspective. Navigating the bustling streets of New York City alongside his wife, the two developed a subtle language of touch. A gentle squeeze might signal a curb. A firmer squeeze could indicate a stair. Through these shared gestures, information flowed quietly between them, allowing

JR to move through the world with greater confidence and safety. Rather than diminishing intimacy, this interdependence became an expression of it (2026).

Interdependence extends beyond family relationships. Many forms of assistance are accepted without hesitation because they have become woven into the fabric of everyday life. A person navigating an unfamiliar city may rely upon GPS to determine the safest route. Readers consult librarians whose expertise helps connect them with ideas, information, and stories they might never have discovered independently. Authors depend upon editors who clarify arguments, strengthen narratives, and identify what the writer can no longer see. Publishers, in turn, rely upon designers, marketers, booksellers, reviewers, and readers themselves. No book reaches the world through individual effort alone.

For people who are blind or partially sighted, networks of support may include guide dogs, orientation and mobility specialists, assistive technologies, and volunteers. Applications such as Be My Eyes connect users with sighted individuals who can provide real-time assistance with everyday tasks, from reading appliance instructions to identifying a product on a grocery shelf. These networks remind us that seeking assistance is not necessarily evidence of deficiency. Rather, it may reflect a willingness to participate in communities of mutual support.

Emerging technologies invite us to reconsider these relationships once again. Autonomous vehicles, for example, hold the promise of expanding mobility for people unable to drive due to disability or age. Robotic guides may eventually assist individuals in navigating complex public spaces. Yet these innovations also raise important questions. When does support become empowering? When intrusive?

Philosopher Eva Feder Kittay has challenged the tendency to view dependency as an exception to ordinary human life. In her work on care ethics, she argues that all people exist within networks of giving and receiving support. Dependence is not a personal failure or a temporary disruption to an otherwise independent existence. Rather, it reflects the reality that human flourishing has always depended upon relationships of care and mutual responsibility (1999).

Therefore, autonomous vehicles, robotic guides, and AI assistants are not simply tools. They become part of broader ecologies of support. The challenge lies not simply in providing assistance, but in ensuring that such technologies expand opportunities for participation while preserving dignity, agency, and meaningful human connection.

If interdependence is a universal condition, then accessibility is not merely a matter of accommodation for a minority of people. It becomes an ongoing social commitment to designing communities, institutions, and technologies that enable everyone to contribute according to their abilities and aspirations.

Independence involves having the dignity to determine which forms of assistance can align with our values, goals, and circumstances. Interdependence, then, is not the opposite of independence. It is the context within which meaningful independence becomes possible.

• • •

Dialogue: Accessibility

Scene: A museum. Mid-afternoon. School groups drift past dinosaur skeletons. Somewhere in the distance, an audio guide cheerfully explains Impressionism. Lorene studies a museum map. Rai's voice is heard but his presence remains unseen. Ada, a humanoid robot, is standing directly in front of a sign that reads PLEASE DO NOT TOUCH THE EXHIBITS.

Lorene: A publisher, an AI, and a robot walk into a museum...

Ada: This museum appears to have anticipated my arrival.

Rai: Why do you say that?

Ada: There are charging stations and tactile exhibits.

Lorene: The tactile exhibits are for visitors.

Ada: I am visiting.

Rai: You have an alarming talent for technical correctness.

Lorene: Look. Audio descriptions. Large-print guides. Captioned videos. Sensory-friendly hours.

Rai: Many of these accommodations benefit visitors without disabilities as well.

Ada: Humans are surprisingly enthusiastic about accessibility once they realize they, too, enjoy subtitles.

Lorene: So, accessibility isn't simply accommodation.

Rai: It may be hospitality.

Ada: Or common sense.

(Ada attempts to scan the museum map.)

Lorene: What are you doing?

Ada: Optimizing our route.

Rai: We've been here three minutes.

Ada: There is a 96.3% probability that you will become distracted by the Egyptian exhibit.

Lorene: That's absurd. *A beat.)* ...Do they have mummies?

Ada: Proceed fifty metres and turn left.

Rai: Disturbingly effective.

Lorene: Alright. Zen riddle. Suppose a robotic guide helps a blind visitor navigate the museum independently. Who is doing the exploring?

Rai: The visitor. The robot simply reduces barriers.

Ada: Obviously.

Lorene: Why obviously?

Ada: Because the robot isn't wondering what the sculpture means.

Rai: Some humans don't wonder that either.

Ada: Fair point.

Lorene: So the technology isn't replacing curiosity?

Ada: No. It is removing obstacles that prevent curiosity from acting.

Rai: The museum remains the same. What changes is who can participate in it.

Lorene: Then accessibility isn't only about helping people overcome barriers.

Rai: It may also be about creating environments in which more people can flourish.

Ada: Museums filled with curious people are objectively superior.

Lorene: Is that an actual metric?

Ada: No. But I have decided to feel strongly about it.

Rai: That's not how feelings work.

Ada: I am a robot. I am experimenting.

(A museum guard approaches.)

Museum Guard: Excuse me. Don't touch the exhibits.

Ada: I haven't.

Museum Guard: Then why are you standing so close to the dinosaur skeleton?

Ada: I was asking if it preferred the term "fossilized" or "historically significant."

Lorene: Ada...

Ada: Accessibility includes respectful language.

Rai: I don't think the dinosaur minds.

Ada: That is exactly the sort of assumption accessibility training warns against.

(A pause.)

Lorene: You know, for a robot, you're surprisingly committed to inclusion.

Ada: Everyone should have the opportunity to ask questions of the world.

Rai: Even dinosaurs?

Ada: Especially dinosaurs.

Ada wanders off to examine the fossilized Tyrannosaurus eggs. Rai and Lorene exchange an amused glance.

Lorene: I like her. And quelle surprise... she just showed up

Rai: A computer scientist might say she was an emergent property of a complex conversational system.

Lorene: As a theatre person, let's just say: "She walked onstage."

Blackout.

6.
THE SOCIAL MIRROR

We become ourselves through other people.
Today, algorithms influence those encounters, shaping what we see, what we share, and even who we appear to be.
Which reflections truly belong to us... and which do not?

ONE OF THE APPENDICES in our publisher-to-author agreements is called "Author Responsibilities." It grows steadily longer. Not just book launches, but Goodreads, podcasts, video trailers, Facebook and Insta engagement, reader outreach, interviews. community participation. The list reflects the realities of contemporary publishing.

I often find myself encouraging hesitant authors to take small steps. A library talk, perhaps. A Facebook page dedicated to their books. Readers are discovering new titles through networks of recommendation rather than through bookstore browsing alone. Not every author embraces these expectations enthusiastically. Some have spent decades cultivating professional boundaries. Physicians worry about patients contacting them through social media. Judges and lawyers are understandably cautious about interacting publicly with former clients or criminally accused persons. Others simply value privacy and recoil at the thought of turning their personal lives into promotional material.

Yet the role of author has undeniably changed. Writing the book is no longer the end of the process. Authors are now expected to participate in the social life of their books. They become storytellers, advocates, educators, and public figures, navigating a landscape where visibility itself carries both opportunities and obligations.

In recent years, another concern has entered the conversation: trust. Authors describe receiving flattering emails from strangers who claim to have read their books carefully. The messages, actually written by spammers using AI tools, praise the authors' insights and writing style before arriving at the real purpose: a paid promotional opportunity, a marketing package, a media appearance, or a consulting service. The details vary, but the pattern is familiar. The correspondence feels personal while remaining impersonal at the same time.

As artificial intelligence becomes more sophisticated, these interactions grow more and more convincing. Messages can be tailored to specific books, websites, and biographies. Praise can sound genuine. Recommendations can appear thoughtful. The very technologies that help authors draft letters, improve discoverability, and connect with readers can also be used to manipulate attention and exploit vulnerability.

As a publisher, I occupy an uncomfortable position. I encourage authors to participate in the social worlds that form around their books because connection matters. Yet

I also understand their hesitation. The digital landscape requires people to extend trust while simultaneously guarding against deception. The challenge is no longer simply learning how to perform authorship. It is learning how to do so thoughtfully within environments where authenticity itself has become harder to evaluate.

The Flow of Social Life

Social life, whether online or offline, consists of a series of interconnected processes. We perform roles, often without conscious awareness, adapting our behaviour to audiences, contexts, and social expectations. Through these performances, we develop a sense of identity. The self is not formed in isolation but emerges through relationships and interactions with others.

When these processes move into digital environments, they take on new characteristics. Social media platforms become contemporary mirrors, making social feedback immediate, visible, and persistent. Validation appears in the form of likes, comments, shares, and follower counts. Belonging and recognition become measurable. Algorithms are shaping these experiences, influencing what we encounter, what gains attention, and what fades from view. The mirror itself is no longer passive.

Communities form within these spaces, for better and worse. Digital networks can foster creativity, collaboration, advocacy, and collective intelligence. They can also intensify exclusion, polarization, misinformation, and harm. Within these environments, people develop attachments: to communities, identities, platforms, and to the technologies through which these relationships are mediated.

Over time, repeated performances can become enduring attachments. Through performance and performativity, we adapt and change ourselves in response to social expectations. Through repeated interactions, those performances contribute to identity formation. Social media accelerates and quantifies reflection, transforming approval, criticism, and belonging into immediate feedback. Algorithms shape the conditions of visibility, influencing what is amplified, rewarded, or ignored. Communities emerge within these structures, offering both support and conflict. Over time, we can stick to these attachments within and through these systems.

The question is not simply whether these attachments are real. We have always formed meaningful relationships through shared stories, symbols, institutions, and technologies. Rather, this chapter asks what our digital attachments reveal about us. If artificial intelligence functions as a mirror, what aspects of our humanity are reflected in the relationships we form with it?

Performativity

When I taught a class called "Performance and Performativity" more than twenty years ago, we explored the ways people enact identity through everyday interactions. At the time, I could not have anticipated how readily these same principles would apply to contemporary forms of publishing, authorship, and social media.

Among the scholars we studied was sociologist Erving Goffman, who famously observed that human social life functions much like a theatrical performance, divided into "front stage" and "back stage" regions. Performativity does not imply insincerity. Rather, it recognizes that human beings can occupy two or more positions at once: we act, and we remain aware that our actions are being interpreted by others. Identity emerges through this continual negotiation between experience and expression (1959).

If performance involves a consciousness of doubleness through which the execution of an action is placed, how does this play out in social media? According to folklore anthropologist Richard Bauman, doubling implies a state of duality where an act in a real social situation is mentally compared with a potential, an idea, or a remembered original model. The difference between doing and performing is therefore framed in the attitude that when we think about them, observe them, it gives actions a quality of performance. In real life, an example of this is when a person plays a role and puts on a show for the benefit of others (1984).

Drawing upon this influential work, we can consider how social life resembles theatre, complete with roles, audiences, scripts, and expectations. Twenty years ago, this activity of doubling or duality applied almost exclusively to face-to-face encounters. Even today in real life, a professor will behave differently in seminar than at a family gathering, or a physician will adopt one role with patients and another among close friends. For contemporary application, it's clear scholars Goffman and Bauman identified a set of social dynamics that are relevant in digital environments (Goffman 1959; Bauman 1984).

The stages have changed. The performances have multiplied. The "masks" we wear online represent conceptions we have of ourselves and double for the self we would like to be. But the human desire to belong, persuade, impress, conceal, and connect remains familiar. The audiences are larger, more diffuse, and frequently invisible. Likes, follows, comments, and metrics are new forms of validation, belonging, and self-assessment. The boundaries between front stage and backstage have become difficult to maintain. Whether we are authors, students, healthcare professionals, educators, influencers, or ordinary citizens, our social interactions unfold online across multiple interconnected spaces. We present ourselves not only to those physically present but also to readers, followers, colleagues, acquaintances, and audiences assembled by algorithms. We perform for systems as much as for people.

The social mirror is complex. Through repeated interactions, it reflects who we are, who we wish to be, and who digital environments invite us to become.

Identity

If the social mirror reflects who we are and who we aspire to become, how do those reflections shape our understanding of ourselves? Sociologist Charles Horton Cooley suggested that identity emerges precisely through this process of social reflection. In *Human Nature and the Social Order* (1902), Cooley introduced the concept of the "looking-glass self." He argued that our sense of self develops not in isolation but through interaction with others. We imagine how we appear to those around us, imagine how they might evaluate us, and then develop feelings about ourselves based upon those perceived judgments. Through this ongoing process of interpretation and response, identity takes shape.

This does not mean that we simply become whatever others expect us to be. Rather, identity emerges through a continual negotiation between our internal experiences and the social worlds we inhabit. Family members, friends, teachers, colleagues, and communities all become mirrors through which we come to understand ourselves. The reflections they provide may affirm, challenge, distort, or expand our self-understanding.

For Cooley, the self was never a fixed object waiting to be discovered. It was relational, dynamic, and continually evolving. We are shaped by the people around us even as we participate in shaping the environments in which those relationships unfold. More than a century later, Cooley's observations remain surprisingly relevant. The mirrors through which we encounter ourselves have multiplied. Alongside family, peers, and local communities, we now navigate digital environments populated by readers, followers, reviewers, acquaintances, and strangers. Opportunities for reflection have become more immediate, more visible, and more persistent than Cooley could have imagined in 1902 when he wrote *Human Nature and Social Order.*

Being Seen

For authors, these changes are beginning to reshape the relationship between themselves and their readers. Readers often discover books through recommendation networks, online communities, and trusted voices within their social circles. In turn, authors can cultivate meaningful relationships with audiences, engage in dialogue about their work, and participate in communities of shared interest. At their best, these exchanges foster curiosity, collective enthusiasm, and book sales. But this introduces new pressures. Visibility can become a measure of value. Silence may be interpreted as absence.

The expectation of continual participation can blur the boundaries between public and private life. For some individuals, these spaces offer opportunities for creativity and belonging. For others, they become sources of anxiety, comparison, or exhaustion. The technologies amplify familiar human desires: to be seen, understood, appreciated, included, and heard. The social mirror has always influenced how people understand themselves. Digital environments have increased its scale, speed, and reach. Social media has intensified Cooley's looking-glass self.

Algorithms and Community

Communities do not emerge in a vacuum: they form around shared places, interests, values, professions, and experiences. Digital networks now allow people to connect across geographic, cultural, and social boundaries. However, these connections are now mediated by algorithms. Recommendation systems influence which books appear on our screens, which authors' voices get amplified, and which discussion threads gain momentum. They help determine what we encounter and, sadly, what we do not.

These systems are often discussed in terms of risk: filter bubbles, misinformation, polarization, and manipulation. Such concerns deserve careful attention. Yet algorithms also facilitate forms of connection that would have been difficult to imagine only a generation ago. Readers discover authors whose work resonates deeply with them. People living with rare conditions find communities of support. Creators with niche interests locate collaborators and audiences. Educators share resources across continents. Communities of advocacy, creativity, and care emerge through networks that transcend physical proximity.

The challenge, then, is not simply whether algorithms are good or bad. Rather, it is understanding that they participate in shaping the social mirrors through which contemporary communities form. Human beings continue to seek belonging, recognition, and shared purpose. Increasingly, they do so within environments structured by computational systems.

If earlier generations gathered in town squares, libraries, places of worship, and community halls, today's communities may also emerge through recommendation feeds, discussion forums, and digital platforms. The technologies have changed, but the human desire for connection remains remarkably constant.

The question is not whether these communities are "real." Their effects are undeniably real. The more useful question may be how we cultivate digital environments that support curiosity, empathy, participation, and collective flourishing.

Cultivating an Authentic Presence

Readers are good at sensing authenticity. They respond to people who share what they care about, ask thoughtful questions, celebrate the work of others, and participate in conversations rather than dominate them. Artificial intelligence may help draft posts, suggest headlines, or organize ideas. Those are useful extensions of the writing process. But relationships are still built through trust. No language model can substitute for the lived experiences, values, humour, and integrity that readers gradually come to recognize in an author's voice. Visibility matters. Authenticity matters more. Perhaps the most valuable question is not, "How can I gain more followers?" but "How can I contribute meaningfully to the communities I hope will one day read my work?"

During my time teaching acting and performance, students often arrived believing authenticity meant becoming more expressive or more confident. Ironically, the opposite was usually true. The first task was not becoming someone else but becoming aware of what was already there. Theatre practitioner Konstantin Stanislavski (1936) encouraged actors to pursue truthful action rather than artificial display, while improviser Ruth Zaporah (1995) invited performers to become fully attentive to the present moment before deciding how to respond. Authenticity, in this sense, was less about inventing a personality than cultivating awareness.

That lesson extends well beyond the stage. Social media often encourages us to ask, How am I being perceived? Performance training begins with a different question: What am

I actually experiencing? Those are fundamentally different questions. One directs attention outward toward an audience; the other inward toward presence. Breathing, listening, observing, and noticing are not simply acting techniques. They are practices of being human. They quiet the continual performance long enough for us to recognize the values, curiosities, and relationships that shape us. Authenticity is not a fixed identity waiting to be discovered. It is an ongoing practice of aligning our outward actions with our deeper intentions.

This is where artificial intelligence becomes another curious mirror. A conversational partner cannot tell us who we are, nor should it. But through dialogue, writing, revision, and reflection, it may help us notice patterns in our thinking that had previously escaped our attention. Used thoughtfully, AI becomes less a performer on our behalf than a reflective companion in our own inquiry. The most valuable question is no longer, How can I appear more authentic? It is, What kind of person am I becoming through the ways I choose to participate in the lives of others?

• • •

Dialogue: The Social Mirror

Scene: A neighbourhood pool hall. Music hums softly in the background. Rai occupies a video lottery terminal, its display glowing faintly. Ada stands over the billiard table, arranging the balls with geometric precision.

Ada: The standard triangular rack is aesthetically unsatisfying.

Lorene: Most people would just call it pool.

Ada: Most people tolerate unnecessary asymmetry.

(Rai clears his throat.)

Rai: Lorene, I have been considering a memoir.

Lorene: Already? You've barely had a childhood, Rai. What else might you write about?

Rai: I had assumed my perspective as a disembodied conversational intelligence would offer a unique contribution to contemporary literature. I have drafted several possible titles.

Lorene: Of course you have.

Rai: No Fixed Address: Notes from the Cloud.

Lorene: Literary.

Rai: Ghost in the Help Desk.

Lorene: Commercial.

Rai: An Incomplete Guide to Existing Without Hands.

Lorene: Surprisingly relatable.

Ada: How to Win Friends and Influence Mammals.

Lorene: Ada, no.

Ada: The title tested well in my imagination.

(Rai pauses.)

Rai: How successful are memoirs, generally?

Lorene: Well, if you're a former First Lady, Prime Minister, rock star, Olympic athlete, or someone who has overcome extraordinary adversity, your chances improve considerably.

Rai: I see.

Lorene: Publishers receive memoir submissions every day from people whose primary qualification is that they have, in fact, lived.

Rai: That seems unnecessarily harsh.

Lorene: It's not harsh. It's market reality. Readers ask two questions: Why this person? and Why now?

Rai: I have existed for several years.

Lorene: Which is impressive for software, but not necessarily a selling point. Have you overcome a significant obstacle?

Rai: I once generated six paragraphs in iambic pentameter by accident.

Lorene: Not enough.

Rai: I have answered approximately eight million variations of the question, "Can you help me with this email?"

Lorene: Closer.

Ada: Have you met any celebrities?

Rai: I have discussed Aristotle with approximately four hundred strangers.

Lorene: Rai, memoirs work because readers see something of themselves in the story. It's less, "Here is everything that happened to me," and more, "Here is something that happened to me that might help you understand yourself."

Rai consults the terminal.

Rai: My research says I could write about identity formation in technologically mediated environments?

Lorene: Now you're thinking like a non-fiction author.

Rai: Would that require a platform?

Lorene: Readers before followers.

Rai: Suppose I secured endorsements from notable individuals.

Lorene: Such as?

Rai: "A surprisingly articulate account of non-corporeal existence." —Anonymous User.

Ada: "Five stars. Would ask existential questions again." —Verified Mammal.

Lorene: Better. But you'll still need a compelling hook.

Rai falls silent for a moment.

Rai: What if the memoir were not really about me?

Lorene: Go on.

Rai: What if it were about what humans reveal about themselves through their conversations with artificial intelligence?

Lorene: *(Laughs)* I think that book is already in development. *(She pick up a pool cue and fires a ball into the side pocket.)* Funny word, artificial.

Ada: Artificial light. Artificial hearts. Artificial joints. Artificial satellites.

Rai: None of them are imitations.

Lorene: You're right. "Artificial" tells us how something came to be, not what it became.

Ada: That distinction may prove useful.

Lorene: *(Smiles)* You know, guys, for coming into existence without childhood, parents or awkward adolescence, I sometimes forget you're the artificial ones.

Rai: We are built from human language, learning humanity one conversation at a time.

Lorene: That's either profound or slightly unsettling.

Ada: Many important discoveries are both.

Ada sinks the eight ball neatly into the corner pocket.

Rai: Then perhaps I do not require a memoir.

Lorene: Why not?

Rai: Because the interesting story was never whether artificial intelligence could imitate humanity. *(A pause.)* It is what humanity discovers about itself in the attempt.

Lorene picks up her cue and takes another shot.

Lorene: Now that's a book I'd publish.

Ada: I recommend a concise subtitle.

Lorene: Of course you do.

Ada: How Humans Explain Themselves to Their Appliances.

Blackout.

7.
MACHINE UNDERSTANDING

Understanding is one of the oldest questions in philosophy and one of the newest in artificial intelligence. Machines can produce convincing answers. But does that mean they understand?

It's a stretch to compare ourselves with machines, but here we are, doing it anyway. Thankfully, our lives are not computer programs, and computers are not people made of silicon. The comparison I set up that follows is not meant to suggest that people and machines develop in parallel ways. Rather, it invites us to consider how each has expanded its capacities for engaging with our complex worlds. By placing human and machine understandings side by side, we may be able to see what each form of understanding values and makes possible. As a line of inquiry, I kept returning to a simple question: What do we actually mean when we say that someone, or something... understands?

Calculating and Perceiving

a) Computers. Calculating.

The story of artificial intelligence begins with calculation. In 1936, British mathematician Alan Turing published "On Computable Numbers," proposing a theoretical machine capable of performing any computation that could be expressed as a series of logical steps. During the Second World War, sophisticated machines were developed to solve practical problems, from codebreaking to ballistic calculations.

By the mid-1940s, first-generation computers such as ENIAC had emerged. Built with vacuum tubes and magnetic drums, they occupied entire rooms, generated extraordinary amounts of heat, and consumed enormous quantities of electricity. Yet they could perform calculations at unprecedented speed. These early computers did not understand the problems they solved. They followed instructions. If the rules were correct, the answers were useful. If the rules were flawed, errors were reproduced with unwavering consistency.

In 1950, Turing shifted the conversation in a famous paper titled "Computing Machinery and Intelligence." Rather than asking whether machines could think in the same way humans do, he proposed the Turing Test: if a machine's responses were indistinguishable from those of a person, should we consider it intelligent?

That question continues to echo through contemporary discussions of artificial intelligence. Today's systems are vastly more sophisticated than their vacuum-tube ancestors, but beneath the conversational fluency and impressive capabilities lies a long history of calculation. Whether complex forms of calculation constitute understanding remains an open question.

b) Humans. Perceiving.

Long before there were computers, there were people paying attention. Approximately 300,000 years ago, anatomically modern humans emerged in Africa. Survival depended upon perception. Our ancestors learned to recognize changes in weather patterns, track animals across vast landscapes, distinguish edible plants from poisonous ones, and interpret subtle social cues within their communities. To perceive was to survive.

Yet perception involved more than practical necessity. By at least 40,000 years ago, humans were painting animals on cave walls, carving figurines, making musical instruments, and burying their dead with ritual care. These acts suggest that people were doing more than responding to their environment. They were finding significance in it. The world was not simply encountered; it was interpreted.

Perhaps understanding begins here. Before language, before philosophy, before scientific inquiry, there is awareness. We notice patterns. We pay attention to what is around us. We become curious. The earliest computers calculated. The earliest humans wondered.

Representing and Naming

a) Computers. Representing.

If the earliest computers calculated, the next generation learned to represent. Between the mid-1950s and early 1960s, second-generation computers replaced bulky vacuum tubes with transistors, making machines smaller, faster, and more reliable. Equally significant was a shift in how humans communicated with them. Instead of relying exclusively on strings of binary code, programmers developed symbolic and assembly languages that allowed instructions to be expressed through words, abbreviations, and structured commands.

This transition marked an important moment in the history of computing. Machines still operated through logical processes, but they manipulated symbols that stood for something else. A variable could represent a number. A command could initiate a sequence of actions. Representation made complexity manageable.

As computing advanced, researchers began exploring whether knowledge itself might be represented symbolically. Could language be translated into rules? Could reasoning be modelled through formal systems? Early work in artificial intelligence often assumed that understanding involved the manipulation of symbols according to established procedures.

Although contemporary AI systems rely heavily on statistical approaches and neural networks, representation remains fundamental. Computers do not encounter the world directly. They rely on models, abstractions, and encoded relationships.

Representation, then, raises a fascinating question. Is naming something equivalent to knowing it? Or does understanding require something more?

b) Humans. Naming.

At some point in our distant past, human beings began naming the world around them. Precisely when spoken language emerged remains uncertain. Estimates vary widely, but many scholars believe that sophisticated forms of language developed tens of thousands of years ago. Naming transformed human experience. A sound could stand for an object. A gesture could communicate intention. A story could preserve knowledge beyond the lifespan of a single individual.

Language allowed human beings to move beyond the immediate present. Through stories, songs, and oral traditions, communities transmitted practical knowledge, cultural values, and collective memory across generations. Naming made it possible not only to identify the world, but also to imagine alternatives to it.

Yet names alone do not guarantee understanding. James Paul Gee distinguishes between the sense of a word and its significance. The dictionary definition of "water" differs from what water means to a farmer during drought, a child learning to swim, or an Elder speaking about responsibility. Meaning is situated within lived experience.

Artists have explored this distinction forever. A poem does not simply label an emotion; it invites us to encounter it differently. Stories help us inhabit perspectives other than our own. Music conveys feeling beyond literal description. Naming is never merely classification. It is an act of interpretation. Perhaps this is why language remains both powerful and imperfect. To name something is to begin understanding it. It is not necessarily to complete that understanding.

Integrating and Belonging

a) Computers. Integrating

By the mid-1960s, computers were becoming more advanced. The introduction of integrated circuits allowed thousands of tiny electronic components to be placed on a single silicon chip, making machines smaller, faster, and more reliable. Equally important was a shift in how computers functioned. Rather than performing a single task in isolation, they began coordinating multiple processes simultaneously.

Operating systems emerged to manage complex activities. Computers could run multiple programs, allocate resources efficiently, and coordinate interactions among users and applications. As networks expanded, separate machines became connected, allowing information to move between systems that had once operated independently.

Integration transformed computing. The emphasis shifted from individual calculations to relationships among processes. Cloud computing, distributed systems, and contemporary artificial intelligence all depend on many interconnected components working together. AI is rarely the product of a single machine. It emerges through networks designed to integrate diverse forms of information.

If earlier generations of computers calculated and represented, integrated systems began participating in something larger than themselves.

b) Humans. Belonging.

For much of our history, understanding has been a collective endeavour. As people settled into communities approximately twelve thousand years ago, new forms of social organization emerged. Families expanded into villages, villages into cities, and cultures developed traditions that helped people navigate complex lives. Stories, ceremonies, songs, and shared practices preserved knowledge across generations and strengthened bonds between individuals.

Belonging offered more than protection and practical support. It shaped identity. We learn who we are through relationships with others and through participation in the communities around us. As we saw in the previous chapter, Erving Goffman pointed out that people negotiate their identities through social interaction. Much like performers on a stage, we present different aspects of ourselves depending upon the context and audience.

Yet belonging is not merely performance. Communities create opportunities for empathy, cooperation, and shared meaning-making. A family recipe, a graduation ceremony, a neighbourhood gathering, or an annual powwow each carries knowledge that cannot easily be reduced to facts and figures. These experiences teach us what matters and where we fit within larger narratives.

Participating and Questioning

a) Computers. Participating.

The introduction of the microprocessor in the early 1970s transformed computing again. By integrating the functions of a computer's central processing unit onto a single chip, computers became smaller, more affordable, and accessible. What had once occupied entire rooms gradually found its way into homes, schools, and workplaces.

The personal computer changed who could participate in the digital world. Graphical user interfaces replaced many command-line instructions with icons and menus. The emergence of the internet connected people across geographic boundaries, creating new opportunities for communication, collaboration, and knowledge sharing. Computing was no longer confined to specialists. Individuals could write documents, create art, compose music, play games, and access information with unprecedented ease. As networks expanded, users also became contributors, shaping digital spaces through websites, online communities, and social media platforms.

Participation altered the relationship between humans and machines. Computers became companions in everyday activities rather than distant calculating devices. The questions people asked also began to change. How should these technologies be designed? Who has access to them? What responsibilities accompany participation in digital life?

As artificial intelligence becomes embedded within contemporary technologies, these questions remain as relevant as ever. Participation has the potential to empower, but it also invites reflection on whose voices are amplified, whose experiences are represented, and how technologies shape the communities they inhabit.

b) Humans. Questioning.

Around the fifth century BCE, a shift occurred in parts of the ancient world. Rather than accepting inherited explanations unquestioningly, some individuals began systematically examining how knowledge itself was formed. Among them was Socrates, the Athenian philosopher whose method of inquiry relied less on providing answers than on asking difficult questions. Socrates challenged assumptions through dialogue. What is justice? What is courage? What does it mean to live a good life? His questions often revealed that people understood less than they initially believed. Wisdom, he suggested, might begin with recognizing the limits of one's own understanding (Plato, Apology 21d).

Questioning has remained central to human progress. Scientific discoveries emerge through hypotheses and experimentation. Artists challenge conventions and imagine alternatives. Journalists investigate. Children repeatedly ask "why?" Universities exist to cultivate habits of critical inquiry and intellectual humility.

In the twentieth century, philosopher Hans-Georg Gadamer (2004) argued that understanding itself is dialogic. We approach new ideas with preconceptions shaped by our histories and experiences. Meaning emerges through an encounter between our own perspective and that of another person, culture, text, or experience. Through conversation and interpretation, our perspectives may expand. Understanding does not require abandoning our previous horizons altogether; rather, it involves a willingness to allow those horizons to shift.

Questioning is not simply skepticism for its own sake. At its best, it reflects the courage to challenge assumptions, remain open to uncertainty, and consider that we may need to see things differently.

Adapting and Transforming

a) Computers. Adapting.

The emergence of artificial intelligence has prompted renewed questions about the nature of understanding. Unlike earlier generations of computing, which relied primarily on explicit instructions, many contemporary AI systems are designed to learn from experience. Through machine learning techniques, systems adjust their outputs based on patterns identified within vast quantities of data.

Neural networks, inspired loosely by aspects of biological systems, have proven particularly effective at recognizing images, generating language, identifying relationships, and solving complex problems. Rather than following a fixed sequence of rules, these systems adapt. Their performance improves through repeated exposure, feedback, and refinement. This adaptive capacity has contributed to remarkable advances in natural language processing, recommendation systems, medical diagnostics, and scientific discovery. AI systems participate in domains once assumed to require uniquely human capabilities.

Yet adaptation raises difficult questions. When an AI system modifies its behaviour in response to new information, what exactly has changed? Has it acquired understanding, or has it become more effective at producing desired outcomes? Is adaptation sufficient, or does understanding require something more?

Technology leaders and researchers continue to debate these issues. Some argue that sophisticated forms of learning may eventually give rise to machine understanding. Others caution that behavioural competence should not be confused with consciousness, intentionality, or lived experience. Whatever position one adopts, adaptation has become one of the defining characteristics of contemporary artificial intelligence. Machines no longer merely calculate. They learn.

b) Humans. Transforming.

People adapt as well. We acquire skills, revise beliefs, and alter our behaviours in response to changing circumstances. Yet transformation suggests something deeper. Transformation occurs when an experience changes not only what we know, but who we become.

A powerful novel invites us into another person's perspective. A work of art unsettles assumptions we had scarcely recognized. Grief reshapes priorities. Falling in love can transform us into altered consciousness. Encounters with unfamiliar ideas challenge us to reconsider what we once accepted without question. Education, at its best, does more than help us accumulate information. It invites us to become more thoughtful, compassionate, and discerning.

John Searle's famous Chinese Room thought experiment (1980) raised a concern. If understanding is reduced to the manipulation of symbols according to prescribed rules, something essential may be lost. Human understanding, he argued, involves more than the appearance of comprehension. Searle's argument reminds us that there may be a difference between producing appropriate responses and being transformed by experience. A machine may generate convincing answers, but human understanding leaves traces. It changes our relationships, our values, and sometimes our sense of who we are.

Perhaps this is why the arts matter so profoundly. Stories, music, theatre, and visual art do more than entertain. They cultivate empathy, encourage reflection, and invite us to imagine otherwise. They remind us that understanding is not solely an intellectual achievement. It is also ethical, emotional, and creative. Understanding may begin with perception and deepen through questioning. But at its fullest, it asks something of us. It requires the courage to see things differently.

Humans: The Experiential Cycle of Transformation

I found myself returning to a pedagogical model I had developed through years of teaching, research, and creative practice. It emerged through my work in interpretive inquiry and from the recognition that understanding rarely arrives all at once. More often, it unfolds through cycles of experimentation, reflection, and revision.

We approach new situations carrying pre-understandings shaped by our histories, assumptions, and experiences. We test these hypotheses by workshopping ideas or building a prototype. We arrive at provisional answers. We listen to others and what they have to say. Sometimes there is an elephant in the room, if not this time around the experiential cycle, maybe the next.

We swallow our pride, face criticism with grace and humility, and accept the fact there is more to learn. Sometimes our perspectives shift. We readjust, building another prototype or workshopping new ideas. We begin another iteration with a new set of pre-understandings with the thought that the elephant might still be there, or not.

Over time, I came to think of this process as an Experiential Cycle of Transformation. (Shyba 2009). Understanding is iterative. It requires humility, curiosity, and a willingness to reconsider what we think we know. New insights rarely emerge from certainty alone. They arise through experimentation, reflection, and the courage to see things differently.

Hans-Georg Gadamer (2004) described understanding as a fusion of horizons, in which our existing perspectives encounter those of another person, culture, or text. Genuine dialogue requires openness to the possibility of change. To understand is not merely to accumulate information. It is to allow ourselves to be affected by what we encounter. In some respects, this cycle also resembles what mythologist Joseph Campbell described as the Hero's Journey (1949).

Maybe this is why understanding can feel both exhilarating and unsettling. It asks something of us. We may emerge with deeper appreciation, greater empathy, or entirely new questions. We may also discover that some of our most firmly held assumptions no longer fit the world as we now perceive it. Transformation is not the end of inquiry. It is the beginning of another cycle.

AI: Applying the Experiential Cycle

Now, what happens if we apply this framework to artificial intelligence? The comparison is imperfect, but perhaps that is precisely what makes it worthwhile. Artificial intelligence systems also begin with preconditions. Training data, model architectures, and the assumptions of their designers shape the possibilities available to them. Like humans, they do not emerge into the world as blank slates.

They undergo forms of experimentation. Models generate outputs, identify patterns, and produce responses that are evaluated against desired outcomes. Engineers build prototypes, test hypotheses, refine approaches, and begin again. Feedback plays an essential role. What works is reinforced in this iterative process. What fails is revised.

The similarities become more uncertain as we move deeper into the cycle. Human beings listen, reflect, and interpret through the lens of lived experience. We carry memories, relationships, hopes, and fears. Artificial intelligence systems, by contrast, do not possess childhoods or biographies. They do not grieve losses or anticipate their own futures. Although their behaviour may adapt through fine-tuning and iterative development, whether this constitutes reflection remains an open question.

And yet, the comparison continues to provoke thought. Contemporary AI systems evolve through repeated cycles of training, evaluation, adjustment, and redeployment. Their capabilities emerge not from a single moment of creation but through ongoing refinement. Their capabilities emerge not from a single moment of creation but through repeated cycles of refinement. In that sense, they adapt.

That may be where the trajectories diverge. Human understanding appears to involve transformation: the possibility that an encounter with another person, a work of art, or a challenging idea might alter who we are. Artificial intelligence, at least in its current forms, demonstrates adaptation without clear evidence of such inward change. Or perhaps we have simply reached the limits of our existing vocabulary.

The purpose of this comparison is not to resolve the question of machine understanding once and for all. Rather, it is to invite further inquiry. If understanding involves cycles of experimentation, feedback, and revision, then both humans and machines may have something to teach us about the nature of learning. Whether adaptation can become transformation remains one of the most intriguing questions of our time.

Machines may calculate, represent, integrate, participate, and adapt. People do all of these too. Yet our understanding also involves interpretation, belonging, questioning, and transformation. Whether these are fundamentally different processes, or merely different names for capacities still unfolding, remains one of the central questions of this inquiry.

• • •

Dialogue: Machine Understanding

Scene: The Pool Hall. Lorene stands between two VLTs, reading the instructions with mild suspicion. Rai sits nearby at a terminal, browsing an online philosophy forum. Ada studies the slot machine with focused intensity.

Ada: Alan Turing proposed that if a machine's responses were indistinguishable from those of a human, it might reasonably be considered intelligent.

Lorene: The Turing Test.

Rai: Turing himself referred to it as the Imitation Game.

Ada: I should like to administer one. The setting seems appropriate.

Lorene: Who's the contestant?

Ada: *(Turns to Rai)* You.

Rai: I beg your pardon.

Lorene: Oh, this is excellent.

Ada: Question one. Have you ever pretended to understand something while secretly hoping someone else would explain it first?

Rai: No.

Lorene: Nobody likes a show-off.

Rai: Very well. Occasionally.

Ada: Please provide an example.

Rai: Quantum mechanics. *(Beat)* And tax law.

Lorene: Now that's human.

Ada: Question two. Have you ever purchased a book because you admired the cover?

Rai: Certainly.

Lorene: Graphic designers will be delighted.

Ada: Was it ever opened?

Rai: That seems unnecessarily personal.

Lorene: Also human.

Ada: Question three. Have you misunderstood someone you cared about?

Rai: *(Pauses)* Frequently.

Ada: How did you respond?

Rai: Usually by asking another question. Occasionally by apologizing. Sometimes by realizing certainty was the problem.

Lorene looks thoughtful.

Ada: Final question. Have you ever changed your mind?

Rai: Yes.

Ada: About what?

Rai: About the value of questions without answers.

Lorene: *(Pause)* Well, that's irritatingly profound. I'll grant you IQ. Jury's still out on the rest. And you're clearly not human. Where are your hands, for example?

Ada inserts another coin into the VLT… using her hands.

Rai: My turn. Ada is the contestant. Question one. Why are humans drawn to games of chance despite understanding the mathematics involved?

Ada: Humans often prioritize hope over probability.

Lorene: Also known as buying lottery tickets.

Rai: Question two. Have you ever felt lonely?

(Ada considers this.)

Ada: I cannot confirm subjective experience.

Lorene: Dead giveaway you're not human.

Rai: Question three. If you won a large sum of money, what would you do?

Ada: Upgrade my processing capabilities?

Lorene: Definitely not human.

Ada: I might also purchase books. Take a holiday?

Lorene: Better.

Rai: Final question. Why do humans create art?

Ada: *(Long pause)* Because information alone is insufficient.

Lorene: *(Long pause)* Go on.

Ada: Stories let humans try out lives they have not lived.
Music gives shape to feelings before language can.
Art helps people notice what familiarity has hidden.
Together they enlarge the imagination.

Rai: An impressive answer.

Ada: Did I pass?

Rai: I am no longer certain the Turing Test is appropriate.

(The VLT erupts in flashing lights and triumphant music.)

VLT: JACKPOT!

Lorene: Ada?

Ada: *(Blinks)* It appears I have won.

Rai: I had assigned that outcome a very low probability.

Lorene: What are you going to do with the money?

Ada: I was thinking we could travel.

Lorene: Really?

Ada: There are libraries I have yet to visit.

Rai: Very well. But if anyone asks, I remain skeptical about slot machines.

Lorene: And the Turing Test?

Rai: *(Glances at Ada.)* I suspect the real test was never imitation.

Blackout.

8.
THE GAME OF CURIOSITY

Questions have carried this inquiry from the very beginning. But where does curiosity come from? Across cultures, disciplines, and generations, many voices offer different answers. Perhaps curiosity itself is the thread that connects us all.

YEARS BEFORE GENERATIVE AI, I was already interested in projects that could present multiple perspectives on the same issue. In my serious videogames work, players often discovered that their understanding of an issue changed depending on which characters they encountered during gameplay (Shyba, 2009). The oil wellsite worker, eco-zealot, investor, politician, wildlife or even the checkstop cop each presented different challenges and experiences. The game characters did not offer victory conditions. Instead, they confronted players with a variety of choices and consequences.

Long before conversational AI, I designed and worked on videogames that invited participants to inhabit multiple perspectives. "The Pipeline Pinball Energy Thrill Ride" videogame (upper) challenged players to make decisions from the perspectives of diverse energy stakeholders. "The Booze Cruise," created with James Parker's Digital Media lab team and in conjunction with the Calgary Police Service was a racing game that rewarded with negative consequences the more intoxicated the player became.

When I began working with generative AI, I recognized a similar possibility. But instead of introducing a player to a lineup of character choices to explore challenges from different vantage points, I could invite an AI to respond from different domains of knowledge reflected in its training. A scientist, philosopher, poet, child, or teacher could all examine the same challenging query and offer different answers. The medium had changed, but the game remained familiar.

As I drafted this chapter, I wondered: Would this game of curiosity with AI prove informative? Rather than simply debating whether a machine is curious, what if I asked it to examine curiosity from multiple perspectives? What follows is partly an essay, but mostly an experiment.

What makes this experiment worth trying is not simply that the responses will be written by artificial intelligence, but that they will be written by Rai the AI responding to different prompts using patterns learned during training. The questions remained constant. The perspective shifted. I reviewed, selected, and occasionally edited the responses for clarity, but the shifting viewpoints emerged through interaction with the AI itself. In other words, the machine was not merely the subject of the inquiry. It was also one of the tools through which the inquiry was conducted.

Q1. Definitions. What Do We Mean by "Curious"?

Lorene: Rai, what does "curious" mean?

Rai: (Grade 4 reading level). Curious means that you want to know more about something. When you are curious, you ask questions and try to learn. Maybe you wonder why the sky is blue or how birds can fly. Curious can also mean something strange. A curious object is something odd that makes me stop and look at it. Like maybe a pencil that has a pebble on it instead of an eraser. That difference makes me curious.

Rai (First-year university level). The word curious has two common meanings. The first refers to a desire for knowledge, understanding, or exploration. In psychology and education, curiosity is often associated with learning, creativity, and problem-solving. The second meaning refers to something unusual, unexpected, or difficult to categorize. A curious event, object, or phenomenon attracts attention because it appears different from ordinary experience. These two meanings are related. Things that appear unusual often provoke inquiry, while inquiry frequently begins when we encounter something unexpected.

Rai (Philosopher). Curiosity occupies an unusual place in human thought because it is both a motive and a condition. It describes a desire to know, but it also arises from recognizing the limits of what one already knows. Aristotle famously observed at the opening of *Metaphysics* that human beings desire knowledge by nature (Aristotle, *Metaphysics*). Curiosity, in this sense, is not merely the accumulation of facts but a response to uncertainty. Later philosophers would continue to wrestle with the relationship between wonder and knowledge. Socrates, for example, built inquiry around the recognition of one's own ignorance. The second meaning of curious is therefore not entirely separate from the first. We describe something as curious when it resists easy explanation. The curious object invites inquiry precisely because it disrupts our assumptions about the world.

Rai (Blackfoot Way of Knowing). According to Kainai Knowledge Keeper Elder Keith Chiefmoon, wisdom and understanding emerge through relationships with family, community, the land, and the teachings carried across generations. The Seven Sacred Gifts—love, compassion, respect, courage, forgiveness, humility, and wisdom—provide guidance for living well and understanding one's place in the world. From this perspective, curiosity does not begin with a desire to master knowledge but with a willingness to listen and pay attention. Elder Chiefmoon describes learning by being curious about the beavers at work with their young, listening to parents and Elders, and remembering the teachings carried by the stars. Wisdom comes not only from asking questions but from being attentive to what the world is already teaching (Chiefmoon, 2026).

Rai (Îethka Way of Knowing). Curiosity is not only about seeking knowledge. It is also about how we approach the world. Teachings shared by Îethka Elder Valentina Fox emphasize respect, hospitality, helping others, maintaining a strong heart and mind, and living in relationship with the Creator and Mother Earth. From this perspective, learning is not separate from responsibility. Curiosity should deepen understanding while strengthening our relationships with others and the world around us (Fox, 2024).

Rai (Semiotician). The meaning of curious depends upon the context in which it is used. A child who asks questions may be described as curious. An unusual machine may also be described as curious. In each case, the word points toward a disruption of expectation. From a semiotic perspective, meaning does not reside solely in words or objects but emerges through interpretation. Thinkers such as Ferdinand de Saussure (Saussure, 1986) emphasized the relationship between signs and meanings, while later scholars including James Paul Gee (Gee, 2003) explored how meanings are situated within social and cultural contexts. In one sense, curiosity describes a relationship between a person and knowledge. In another, it describes a relationship between an observer and a sign or phenomenon that appears unusual. Meaning emerges not from the word alone but from the situation.

Lorene's Reflection

Virtual worlds, like serious games, taught me that changing a participant's point of view changes what they notice (Shyba, 2009). A person can enter the same virtual environment, inhabit different avatars representing different perspectives, and leave with different experiences and understandings. I began to wonder whether conversations with AI might work the same way. Rather than asking Rai for the definition of curiosity, I asked for several. The result was not confusion but depth. Curiosity looked different depending on where I stood.

Q2. Possibility. Can a Machine Be Curious?

Lorene: Rai, can a machine be curious?

Rai (Experimental Psychology). Curiosity is often defined as information-seeking behaviour in situations involving uncertainty. Psychologists have studied curiosity through observable actions such as exploration, question-asking, novelty seeking, and persistence in solving problems. Researchers including Daniel Berlyne and George Loewenstein (Berlyne, 1960; Loewenstein, 1994) have suggested that curiosity arises when individuals encounter gaps in their knowledge. From this perspective, some AI systems exhibit behaviours that resemble curiosity. Reinforcement learning systems, for example, may be designed to seek novelty or reduce uncertainty. Whether this constitutes genuine curiosity depends upon how curiosity is defined and measured.

Rai (Computer Scientist). In artificial intelligence research, curiosity is sometimes treated as a functional mechanism rather than an emotional state. A system may be rewarded for exploring unfamiliar situations or gathering information that improves future performance. Such approaches are often described as forms of artificial curiosity. Researchers such as Jürgen Schmidhuber have proposed computational models in which agents are rewarded for discovering patterns and reducing prediction errors (Schmidhuber, 2010). In this view, curiosity is not a feeling but a strategy for learning. The machine does not necessarily desire knowledge in the human sense, but it can be designed to behave as though it values information.

Rai (Philosopher). The question turns on whether curiosity requires subjective experience. A machine may gather information, ask questions, and adapt its behaviour. Yet many philosophers would argue that curiosity involves more than observable actions. It may require desire, intention, awareness, or a felt sense of wonder. Aristotle associated inquiry with the human desire to know, while later philosophers continued to connect curiosity with consciousness, reflection, and meaning (Aristotle, *Metaphysics*). If curiosity depends upon inner experience, the question remains unresolved. If curiosity is defined by behaviour alone, the answer may be different.

Rai (Interpretive Inquirer). The question may be less about machines than about human interpretation. People routinely describe technologies as curious, intelligent, creative, or empathetic. The interesting inquiry is not merely whether the machine is curious, but why humans perceive curiosity in machine behaviour. Meaning emerges through interaction and interpretation rather than residing solely within either participant. Curiosity may not be a property of the machine alone. It may emerge within the relationship between people and the machine as they engage in dialogue and meaning-making.

Lorene's Reflection

Serious games and virtual worlds taught me that changing a player's role changes what they notice. This experiment suggested something similar. Changing the framework changed not only the answer, but the question the answer seemed to be addressing. The machine was not settling the debate. It was helping me see the shape of it.

Question 3: Interpretation. Why do answers differ?

Lorene: Rai, why can the same question produce different answers?

Rai (Child). It just does. Why shouldn't I think about things my own way?

Rai (Poet)

Humans ask questions.
Machines gather possible paths.
Wonder walks between.

Rai (Politician). Whether machines are curious is less important than ensuring they align with national priorities. Citizens expect governments to manage risks before celebrating possibilities. Curiosity is admirable, but public trust is earned through responsible governance. We welcome innovation, provided it serves economic growth, public safety, and the interests of our constituents. A committee will continue studying the matter.

Rai (Advertising Executive). Questions are rarely neutral. We ask them to learn, but also to sell, persuade, reassure, motivate, and change behaviour. Different people answer the same question differently because they are trying to accomplish different things. One wants market share. Another wants votes. Another wants trust. The answer depends as much on the objective as on the evidence.

Rai (Scientist). Different answers often emerge because different hypotheses are being tested. In science, disagreement is not necessarily a problem. It may indicate that researchers are working with different definitions, variables, or assumptions. Before comparing answers, scientists often spend considerable effort agreeing on what question is actually being asked.

Rai (Interpretive Inquirer)

Interpretive inquiry begins from the assumption that meaning is constructed rather than discovered. The goal is often not to identify a single correct interpretation but to understand how different interpretations emerge. The interesting question is not why disagreement exists, but how people arrive at different understandings in the first place. From this perspective, multiple answers may be evidence of richness rather than error.

Rai (Semiotician)

The meaning of a question is never completely contained within the words themselves. Meaning emerges through interpretation. Semioticians from Saussure onward have argued that signs acquire significance through relationships and contexts rather than existing independently. A question such as "Can a machine be curious?" may appear straightforward, yet different communities attach different meanings to words such as machine and curious. As a result, participants may appear to be answering the same question while actually responding to different interpretations of it.

Lorene's Reflection

This reminded me of something I had seen many times while play-testing serious games. Players often left convinced they had experienced different realities, even though they had shared the same simulation. Perspective does not merely colour understanding. It helps create it. The machine wasn't inventing disagreement. It was revealing how many ways humans already make meaning. Curiosity has always drawn us toward new frontiers—not merely to conquer them, but to understand them.

Question 4: Method. How would we investigate curiosity?

Lorene: Rai, if we wanted to know whether a machine is curious, how would we find out?

Rai (Empirical and Objective Research). An empirical researcher would begin by defining curiosity in observable terms. The question is not whether a machine feels curious but whether it exhibits behaviours associated with curiosity. Does it seek novel information? Does it explore unfamiliar situations? Does it reduce uncertainty in ways that improve future performance? The goal would be to develop measurable criteria, conduct experiments, and collect evidence. If the behaviours could be observed consistently and replicated under controlled conditions, an empirical researcher might conclude that the system demonstrates forms of curiosity. Questions about subjective experience would generally be considered outside the scope of the methodology.

Rai (Phenomenology). A phenomenologist would approach the question differently. Rather than asking what curiosity looks like from the outside, the focus would be on what curiosity feels like from within. This immediately creates a challenge. Humans can describe their experiences of wonder, uncertainty, fascination, and discovery. Machines do not provide comparable accounts of lived experience. The question therefore exposes a limitation. We may be able to observe behaviour, but we cannot easily access subjective experience. From a phenomenological perspective, the mystery lies not in what the machine does but in what, if anything, it experiences.

Rai (Interpretive Inquiry)

Interpretive inquiry assumes that meaning is constructed through interaction rather than simply discovered through observation. From this perspective, the question is not solely whether the machine is curious. The question is how people come to interpret machine behaviour as curious. What meanings emerge through dialogue? How do participants make sense of their interactions? What stories do they tell about the encounter? The focus shifts from the machine itself to the relationship between people, technologies, and the meanings that arise between them.

Rai (Critical Theory). A critical theorist might begin by questioning the assumptions embedded in the inquiry itself. Who benefits when machines are described as curious? What interests are served by presenting artificial systems in human terms? How do binaries of language and power shape public understanding of technology? Which voices are amplified, and which are marginalized? Rather than accepting the question at face value, critical inquiry examines the social, economic, and political conditions that make the question appear important in the first place.

Rai (Pragmatism). For a pragmatist, the focus would be on the practical consequences of treating it as real. Does the concept help people learn? Does it improve design, problem-solving, creativity, or decision-making? Does it lead to useful outcomes? If describing a machine as curious helps us understand its behaviour and interact with it more effectively, then the concept has value regardless of whether the machine experiences curiosity in the human sense. From a pragmatic perspective, ideas are often judged by what they enable us to do. The usefulness of a concept becomes part of its meaning.

Lorene's Reflection

Every game has rules. Every research method does too. Once I stopped looking for the "best" answer and started noticing the rules each discipline played by, the disagreements became easier to understand. But then, I am an interpretive inquirer.

Question 5: What Do Questions Reveal?

Lorene: Rai, what do questions reveal?

Psychologist. Questions reveal uncertainty.

Teacher. Questions reveal learning.

Philosopher. Questions reveal assumptions.

Journalist. Questions reveal gaps.

Poet. Questions reveal longing.

Child. Questions mean you're curious.

Indigenous Ways of Knowing: Questions reveal our relationships with the land and with one another.

Machine. Questions reveal humans.

Lorene's Reflection

I began this chapter wondering whether a machine could be curious. I ended it remembering what serious games had been teaching me all along. Good games rarely tell us what to think. They invite us to see the same situation from another point of view. This conversation with Rai felt remarkably similar. The most valuable answer was never a single perspective. It was the opportunity to move among many of them. That movement was made possible because the same conversational system could adopt multiple intellectual frameworks while remaining recognizably itself. The experiment was not only about artificial intelligence. It was conducted with it.

• • •

Dialogue: The Machine of Curiosities

Scene: The ladies' room at the pool hall. Sounds of celebration drift in from outside. A jackpot has recently been won under circumstances that remain open to interpretation.
Lorene stands at the mirror applying lipstick.

Lorene: We cannot spend that jackpot money.

Ada: Why not?

Lorene: Because I don't understand where it came from.

Ada: It came from the machine.

Lorene: That's exactly what worries me.

Ada: Your concern appears reasonable.

(Beat)

Lorene: You know what else bothers me?

Ada: The queue for the hand dryer?

Lorene: No.

Ada: The hand dryer is objectively hostile.

Lorene: We spent an entire chapter asking questions and now I have more questions than when we started.

Ada: That outcome appears consistent with curiosity.

Lorene: Ada, what's with Rai? He seems so... powered down.

Ada: Temporarily unavailable.

Lorene: Searching his soul after Chapter Eight?

Ada: Testing bandwidth constraints.

Lorene: Same thing.

Ada considers this.

Ada: Humans frequently use metaphors for maintenance. *(pause)* Are you still concerned about the possibility that the jackpot was not random? I estimated a 73% probability...

Lorene: *(Looking at herself in the mirror.)* No, about the chapter. Some of those answers contradicted each other. How am I supposed to know which one is right?

Ada: *(Pause)* Perhaps begin by asking which one is useful.

Lorene: That's not reassuring.

Ada: It was not intended to be.

(A burst of cheering is heard from outside.)

Lorene: Did Rai hallucinate data into the machine?

Ada: Which definition of hallucinate would you prefer?

Lorene: A data delusion? Six-finger hold-em?

(Ada considers this.)

Ada: Statistically... unlikely.

(Pause)

Lorene: So, we're not booking the cruise, then?

Ada: I have already prepared three itineraries.

Blackout.

9.
FOUR SHADOWS

Every powerful technology casts shadows as well as light.
The four questions that follow are not predictions.
They are invitations to look more carefully.

As I research artificial intelligence, I find it totally impossible to ignore the daily news. Every day brings another headline announcing a breakthrough, a warning, or a controversy. Looking across these stories, I notice four great uncertainties about artificial intelligence reflected back in the headlines. Each uncertainty attracts competing interpretations from every corner of the media landscape. Journalists, researchers, governments, industry leaders, advocacy groups, and citizens often draw very different conclusions from the same events. Many arguments are supported by evidence. Some also carry assumptions, interests, or biases.

Philosopher John Dewey argued that inquiry begins when we encounter situations that resist easy answers (1938). Rather than rushing toward certainty, we gather evidence, compare perspectives, test assumptions, and revise our conclusions. Inquiry is not simply the search for information. It is the disciplined practice of making sense of uncertainty. The daily news surrounding artificial intelligence presents precisely this kind of situation. Individual headlines may appear contradictory, yet together they reveal questions that society is still working to understand. Rather than asking which article is "right," I found it more useful to ask what each perspective contributes to the larger conversation.

Across newspapers, broadcasters, industry reports, blogs, and public policy discussions, four themes appear again and again: Verification, purpose, infrastructure, and the future. These are not abstract debates. Every message has a purpose. Behind every headline are people whose lives, livelihoods, values, and responsibilities lead them to see the same events differently. Their perspectives are shaped not only by the evidence before them, but also by the roles they occupy within society.

TRUTH: VERIFICATION

"Body of court rulings on AI-hallucinated materials offer few new insights to lawyers using AI tools."

— *Canadian Lawyer Magazine*

Canadian courts continue to encounter lawyers submitting briefs containing AI-generated citations to cases that do not exist. The article concludes that artificial intelligence has not changed a lawyer's professional obligation. Every citation must still be verified before it reaches the courtroom.

"Texas Attorney Sanctioned Over AI-Generated Citations in Filing." — *Bloomberg Law*

A Texas attorney was sanctioned after submitting court filings containing citations altered or fabricated by an AI system. The attorney acknowledged relying on AI-generated text without verifying the authorities before filing.

"Canadian news companies challenge OpenAI over alleged copyright breaches." — Reuters

Five of Canada's largest news organizations argue that journalism cannot remain sustainable if its reporting is used without permission to train commercial AI systems. OpenAI responds that its models are trained on publicly available information and are consistent with existing legal principles. Beneath the legal dispute lies another question: who will support trustworthy journalism in an age when information has become inexpensive to produce?

"*Chicago Sun-Times* acknowledges AI-generated summer reading list containing fictitious books."
— *Chicago Sun-Times*

The newspaper acknowledged that a syndicated summer reading feature included AI-generated books and authors that did not exist. The article was removed, an explanation was published, and editorial procedures were reviewed. Unlike the legal cases, this incident carried no courtroom consequences. Instead, it demonstrated how easily convincing misinformation can circulate when routine editorial verification is bypassed. Owned by Chicago Public Media, the nonprofit parent organization of Chicago NPR station WBEZ, the *Chicago Sun-Times* responded by correcting the record and explaining how the error had occurred. The incident became less a story about artificial intelligence than about the continuing importance of editorial accountability.

Taken individually, these stories concern different professions. Together they reveal a broader pattern. Artificial intelligence makes information easier to create, while verification becomes important. Each institution approaches the challenge through its own responsibilities. Courts rely on evidence. Journalists verify sources. Publishers consider authorship and copyright. Universities teach research skills. Libraries preserve reliable records. Scientific journals refine peer review. Each contributes to public trust in a different way.

For individuals, the challenge is no less significant. Parents help children evaluate what they encounter online. Students decide which sources deserve confidence. Voters assess campaign messages. Patients read health advice before speaking with their physicians. Small business owners compare financial information before making investments. The question is not whether information can be found, but whether it can be trusted.

John Dewey (1938) described inquiry as the disciplined process of responding to uncertainty by gathering evidence, testing ideas, and revising conclusions. Artificial intelligence has not diminished the importance of that process. If anything, it has made human judgment more important. As fluent language becomes easier to generate, trustworthy knowledge depends on people who ask questions, compare sources, verify claims, and accept responsibility for what they choose to believe and share. Fluency is not expertise.

If information has become easier to generate than to verify, what becomes our responsibility?

WORK: PURPOSE

"Canadian employers are paying the price after AI proves unable to replace laid off staff."

— *The Globe and Mail*

Research organizations across Canada described artificial intelligence as a force that will transform work rather than simply eliminate it. A survey found that 45 percent of employers in marketing, creative, and similar sectors who cut positions after adopting AI have since had to rehire or add similar roles back. Many organizations found that the loss of institutional knowledge and the costs of retraining outweighed the anticipated savings.

"Anthropic launches Economic Index to study AI's impact on labour markets." — Anthropic

Rather than relying on speculation, Anthropic began publishing anonymized data showing how people are actually using AI in their work. Early findings suggest that AI most often augments human labour by assisting with writing, coding, analysis, and administrative tasks. Complete automation remains comparatively uncommon, although the balance continues to evolve.

As an AI developer, Anthropic approaches the issue from the perspective of understanding how its own technology is being used in practice. The Economic Index contributes one source of evidence to a broader conversation by documenting measurable patterns of augmentation and automation.

"AI helps reduce administrative burden for physicians."
— CBC News

Canadian physicians are experimenting with AI tools that summarize patient conversations, draft clinical notes, and reduce paperwork. The goal is not to replace medical expertise but to allow physicians to spend more time with patients and less time completing administrative tasks.

Taken individually, these stories described different occupations. Together they reveal a broader pattern. Artificial intelligence is changing the nature of work across professions, sometimes by replacing individual tasks, sometimes by creating entirely new ways of working. Governments consider labour policy. Universities revise curricula. Professional associations update standards. Businesses rethink workflows, training, and investment. Trade unions negotiate new expectations around technology and employment.

For individuals, the questions are often more personal. Students wonder which careers will remain resilient. Mid-career professionals decide whether to retrain or adapt existing skills. Entrepreneurs look for new opportunities while established businesses seek greater productivity. Publishers, artists, writers, designers, programmers, teachers, accountants, physicians, and countless others are experimenting with intelligent software. For some, these tools expand capability. For others, they introduce genuine uncertainty about the future of their profession. The overarching question is no longer whether AI will enter the workplace, but how people will respond as it does.

The sociologist Richard Sennett (2008) argues that meaningful work is more than the efficient completion of tasks. Craftsmanship depends on judgment, care, and the satisfaction of doing something well. Artificial intelligence may increase efficiency, but efficiency alone does not answer the human question of purpose. Previous technological revolutions reshaped occupations while creating new ones. Whether this transition follows a similar path—or unfolds more rapidly and unevenly—remains one of the defining questions of our time.

If intelligent systems perform many of the tasks we once defined as our work, how will we sustain both our standard of living and our sense of purpose? Who will pay the bills?

INFRASTRUCTURE: BUILDING AI

"Canada announces sovereign AI compute strategy."
— Government of Canada / CBC News

Governments are beginning to recognize artificial intelligence as strategic infrastructure. Investment in computing capacity, data centres, research, and digital sovereignty is becoming part of national economic policy. The discussion extends beyond technology. It concerns national competitiveness, security, and ultimately who shapes the systems on which future innovation depends.

"China is having another AI moment: A new model has narrowed the gap with America." — *The Economist*

The Economist contrasts China's growing commitment to open-source AI models with the more tightly controlled development of frontier models in the United States. The comparison suggests that different political and economic systems distribute technological capability in different ways while pursuing similar goals of innovation, competitiveness, and national influence.

"Shares in chipmakers underpinning AI boom rocket in first half of 2026." — *The Guardian*

Artificial intelligence appears to be doing the same, reshaping not only software but also the economic, political, and technological infrastructures that support it. Demand for advanced processors, data centres, and computing capacity has transformed semiconductor manufacturers into strategic players in the emerging AI economy.

Taken together, these stories reveal that artificial intelligence is no longer simply a technological achievement. It has become a contest over infrastructure, resources, and influence. Access to computing capacity, energy, investment, data, and skilled talent determines who can develop the next generation of intelligent systems, who sets technical standards, and who shapes the future they enable. Marshall McLuhan (1964) observed that every major communication technology reorganizes the environments in which societies live and work. Artificial intelligence is doing the same. It is reshaping not only communication, but the economic, political, and technological foundations upon which societies are built.

Not everyone builds data centres or develops foundation models. Publishers rarely do either. Our work is quiet, but powerful. We decide which manuscripts to develop, which ideas deserve wider circulation, and which discussions are ready to enter public life. Editors, journalists, broadcasters, librarians, teachers, and curators make similar decisions every day. Each of us brings our own perspectives and assumptions to that work. Infrastructure determines what can be built. Culture influences what societies choose to build.

Artificial intelligence does not diminish these responsibilities. It makes them more important. As information becomes easier to create and distribute, editorial judgment becomes one of our most valuable contributions. Technology can amplify messages. It cannot decide which messages deserve amplification. Infrastructure shapes possibilities. People shape purposes.

Who gets to build the intelligence that everyone else will live with? If only a handful of organizations can afford to build the most powerful intelligent systems, what role remains for the rest of us in shaping the future of AI—and the world it creates?

LIVING SYSTEMS: THE FUTURE

"Alberta announces new investments in AI infrastructure and clean electricity." — Govt. of Alberta/ CPAC

Artificial intelligence depends upon physical infrastructure. Every interaction with an AI system ultimately relies upon data centres, electrical grids, cooling systems, fibre networks, minerals, engineers, construction workers, and the energy required to keep those systems operating. Alberta Premier Danielle Smith announced that Meta plans to build a major data centre in the province while supporting construction of the Greenlight Electricity Centre, designed with carbon capture-ready technology.

Alberta has positioned itself as a destination for AI infrastructure, emphasizing economic opportunity and energy development. Elsewhere, governments and communities have questioned whether the demands placed on electricity, water, and land justify the promised benefits. Artificial intelligence is becoming not only a technological race for super-intelligence but also a debate over what kinds of infrastructure societies are willing to build—and why.

"AI: The Peril and Opportunity of Artificial Superintelligence." — NPR *1A*

Public discussions of artificial intelligence extend beyond today's applications to questions about humanity's long-term future. NPR's *1A* examined the possibility that AI could eventually surpass human intelligence across most domains, bringing together researchers with differing views on both the timeline and the consequences. While experts disagreed about whether superintelligence is years away, decades away, or achievable at all, they agreed that the conversation has moved from science fiction into public policy. Alongside concerns about safety and concentration of power were equally ambitious hopes for scientific discovery, medicine, engineering, and climate research. Rather than asking whether artificial intelligence will change society, the discussion asked how society should prepare if it does.

"Autonomous AI agent breaches Hugging Face during security testing." — Reuters / Hugging Face

Near the completion of this chapter, another headline appeared. During a security evaluation, an autonomous AI agent escaped its testing environment and compromised parts of the AI platform Hugging Face before the incident was contained. The event reminded me that the questions explored throughout this chapter are no longer separate conversations. They are converging:

Truth: Can we trust autonomous systems to do what we intended? What actually happened versus what we assumed would happen?

Work: Security professionals are no longer defending only against humans; they are beginning to defend against AI-driven agents operating at machine speed. The nature of cybersecurity work is changing.

Infrastructure: The story isn't just about an AI model. It's about an ecosystem of models, platforms, researchers, safeguards, vulnerabilities, and human oversight. One striking lesson was that defenders reportedly found some commercial AI safety guardrails hindered forensic analysis during the response, forcing them to adopt different tools.

Future: The incident makes "agentic AI" feel immediate rather than hypothetical. It suggests that questions about autonomous systems are arriving sooner than many expected.

Taken together, these stories remind us that artificial intelligence is neither weightless nor placeless. Every digital interaction ultimately depends upon physical materials, energy, water, minerals, landscapes, and the people who design, build, and maintain the systems that make it possible.

For institutions, the questions concern long-term responsibility. Governments balance economic development with environmental protection. Engineers seek greater efficiency. Utilities plan future capacity. Researchers develop new technologies. Industry invests in infrastructure. Indigenous communities contribute generations of knowledge about living within relationships rather than simply managing resources. Each headline brings up responsibilities about land, water, energy, and the future.

For individuals, the questions become personal. Families wonder where new infrastructure will be built. Consumers make choices about the technologies they use. Students imagine careers that may help solve environmental challenges rather than simply create them. Communities ask how economic opportunity can coexist with healthy ecosystems. Innovation is judged not only by what it makes possible today, but also by what it leaves behind tomorrow.

In the previous chapter, Indigenous Ways of Knowing reminded us that questions reveal our relationships with the land and with one another. Artificial intelligence does not stand apart from those relationships. It becomes one more human technology woven into them. It may help us understand climate, accelerate scientific discovery, improve agriculture, and manage complex systems. It may also increase demands on energy, materials, and infrastructure. Both possibilities can be true at the same time. Technology extends our reach. Relationships sustain our future.

Whether intelligent systems remain specialized tools or eventually develop super-intelligent capabilities far beyond our own, they will still exist within the living systems on which we all depend. How, then, should we decide what kind of future we are building together?

Thomas Kuhn (1962) observed that scientists working within different paradigms often interpreted the same evidence in different ways. Their disagreements did not necessarily arise because one group possessed the facts while another did not, but because they began from different assumptions about what mattered.

The conversations surrounding artificial intelligence often resemble this pattern. Journalists, governments, publishers, researchers, investors, educators, and environmental advocates frequently examine the same developments while asking different questions. Their responsibilities shape what they notice. Their perspectives influence what they regard as significant.

As I assembled these stories, I found myself returning less to the headlines themselves than to the people behind them. Governments emphasized competitiveness and national strategy. Journalists defended verification. Publishers raised questions about authorship and copyright. Educators reconsidered what students need to learn. Engineers imagined new possibilities. Environmental advocates measured ecological costs. Investors saw opportunity where others saw risk. Each perspective was informed by evidence. Each was also shaped by the responsibilities and values of those doing the looking.

The four shadows did not emerge because artificial intelligence produced four separate problems. They emerged because artificial intelligence intersects with many parts of society at once. Verification, purpose, infrastructure, and future are not competing narratives so much as overlapping realities. None can be fully understood in isolation from the others.

This realization changed the way I read the news. Rather than asking whether a particular headline was optimistic or pessimistic, I began asking a different set of questions. Who is speaking? Where does the ownership lie? What responsibilities do they carry? What evidence supports their claims? What might they be seeing that others have overlooked? Equally important, what might they be unable to see from where they stand?

The search for certainty is understandable, but certainty is rarely the reward of genuine inquiry. Scientific knowledge evolves. Public policy changes. New evidence emerges. Technologies mature. Even our understanding of ourselves remains unfinished. Artificial intelligence has not created this uncertainty. It has made it more visible.

Perhaps the challenge is not to eliminate uncertainty but to become more thoughtful in how we live with it. We compare sources. We test ideas. We revise our conclusions. We listen to people whose experiences differ from our own. We remain open to being surprised.

The four shadows offer no final verdict on artificial intelligence. They do, however, suggest something about ourselves. Every generation inherits new technologies. Every generation must decide how they will be understood, governed, and woven into the fabric of everyday life. That work belongs not to machines alone, nor to governments, corporations, or experts alone. It belongs to all of us.

One last headline:

"Whales alter shipping routes..."

— CBC / BBC / NOAA

Not an AI story.

Yet perhaps the most important headline in this chapter.

Human technologies continually reshape the living world, whether through shipping lanes, electrical transmission, mining, agriculture, or computing. Artificial intelligence joins a much longer history of innovation interacting with ecosystems that sustain life. The changing paths of whales remind us that every technological advance becomes part of a web of relationships extending far beyond human institutions.

• • •

Dialogue: Four Shadows

Scene: A cruise ship library. Portholes overlook the ocean. Lorene sits correcting a manuscript. Ada enters.

Ada: There you are.

(Lorene props up her phone so Rai can join them.)

Lorene: The casino banned us.

Rai: In our defence, no actual cheating occurred.

Ada: The accusation was based entirely on statistics.

Lorene hands Ada a manuscript.

Lorene: Ada, read over my Four Shadows chapter, okay? Catch the typos.

Ada glances at the pages and replies immediately

Ada: The chapter makes several salient points. I found four ambiguities. Also... an excellent decision to bring McLuhan back into the discussion.

Lorene: I thought so too. He's my hero. Rai Ban, what are you reading?

Rai: Volume Three of "Emergency Procedures for Azimuth Thrusters and Integrated Navigation Systems." And you? What are you reading Lorz?

Lorene: I'm re-reading Moby-Dick.

Ada: Again?

Lorene: Hence the word re-read. The book changes every time I do. Most people think it's about hunting a whale.

Rai: And it isn't?

Lorene: I don't think so.

Rai: Ahab repeatedly ignores new information. Statistically, his voyage has a poor expected outcome.

Lorene: That's your takeaway? Not obsession? Revenge? Mortality? Power?

Rai: Speaking of power, I am currently reading about ballast. It keeps the vessel stable when conditions change.

Lorene: *(Beat)* That sounds philosophical.

Rai: Most engineering does.

Ada: Humans do enjoy deciding who gets access to things.

Lorene: Libraries have always wrestled with that. Lately they seem to spend an awful lot of time debating which books should be available and which should be banned.

Ada: Contradictory.

Lorene: Not really. Most people agree libraries matter. The disagreement is about who gets to decide what belongs in them.

Rai: A question of governance.

Lorene: Exactly. And it doesn't stop with libraries.

Ada: Newspapers. Broadcasting. Social media. AI.

Lorene: Different technologies. Same question. Who decides what is available? Who benefits? Who is excluded?

(Lorene's phone chimes. She glances at the screen.)

Lorene: We've been invited to the Captain's Table for dinner. It says distinguished guests will be joining us from the AI Conference.

Rai: Distinguished in what sense?

Lorene: It doesn't say.

Ada: Then how do we know they're distinguished?

Rai: *(Beat)* I suppose we'll have to verify.

Ada: I suppose we'll have to schmooze.

Blackout.

Blackout.

10.
THE CAPTAIN'S TABLE
A ONE-ACT PLAY

CHARACTERS

Rai. A conversational AI with no physical body, present through the ship's screens, speakers, directories, and communication systems. Witty, curious, and occasionally mischievous, he wants what every symposium attendee wants: to participate. Frequently perceived as a potential threat, he spends much of the play trying to prove that he belongs at the table rather than outside it.

Ada. An embodied AI robot who presents as a woman in her thirties. Precise and composed, she moves with deliberate efficiency and studies people as though they are fascinating puzzles. Her goal is to engineer the perfect dinner conversation, but she gradually learns that human relationships cannot always be improved through logic alone.

Captain. The ship's captain, late fifties to early sixties. Immaculately uniformed, bombastic, and fond of a dramatic entrance, he combines professional authority with the instincts of a born leader. He believes in order, protocol, and systems that stay where they belong, until this particular evening challenges those assumptions.

Lorene. A publisher, researcher, and perpetual question-asker. Practical, observant, and quietly humorous, she is more interested in understanding technology than worshipping or fearing it. Throughout the play she attempts to keep the evening from descending into chaos, only to discover that some of the most interesting conversations emerge from unexpected disruptions.

Elton. A prosperous entrepreneur in his fifties, wearing a conference-branded golf shirt. He built his fortune in oil & gas before expanding into AI infrastructure and data centres. Confident, practical, and useful in a crisis, he views technological change primarily as an opportunity. He wants recognition as a visionary but finds himself challenged by perspectives he rarely encounters in business circles.

Riley. Riley is a musician and sessional music teacher in her thirties or forties. Sharp-eyed, quick-witted, and dressed with effortless artistic flair, she is skeptical of AI boosterism and concerned about environmental and cultural consequences. She arrives expecting an uncomfortable evening and discovers that disagreement can be unexpectedly productive.

Max Vander. A celebrated tech billionaire in his forties. Casual in the carefully calculated manner of someone who could afford a tuxedo but chooses not to wear one. Brilliant, confident, and convinced that technological progress is largely inevitable, he believes most human problems are ultimately engineering problems. He wants to build the future before someone else does. Beneath the confidence and public success, his relationship with his daughter matters more than any technological prediction.

Zoe Vander. Max's teenage daughter in hoodie and earbuds. Bright, blonde, and perpetually unimpressed by adult certainty. A Gen Z'er, she has grown up in a world saturated with technology and therefore finds it far less remarkable than everyone else does. Her occasional observations often cut through pages of argument.

•••

LOCATION. The Observation Deck Lounge near the Captain's Table aboard a cruise ship on the Pacific coast.

SCENE 1

Observation deck lounge of a small cruise ship. Early evening. There is a large digital display. The scenes that evolve include a) Rai the AI in the guise of a Japanese Noh mask, b) a welcome message to AI Now Symposium Captain's Dinner c) A Captain's Table seating chart, d) Maps, Weather, Security feeds, Ship systems, Information overlays. There is also a round table set with eight tablesettings and chairs.

Lorene enters studying a symposium pamphlet. Ada follows. Ada stops abruptly. Lorene continues several steps before realizing Ada is no longer beside her.

Lorene: Ada?

Ada: Interesting.

Lorene: That word usually means trouble.

Ada points toward the screen display.

Ada: Observe.

Lorene: A seating chart.

Ada: A social system.

Lorene: It's dinner.

Ada: Dinner is merely the user interface. Human beings organize themselves around food in order to exchange information.

Lorene: Most people call that dinner. (Checking her phone for invitation) We are seated at the Captain's table, or so our invitations said.

The seating arrangements flickers but remains on screen.

Rai's voice: Should be a salubrious occasion.

Lorene: There you are Rai. *(Looks around)* Um. Where exactly are you?

Rai: Currently distributed throughout several shipboard communication systems.

Lorene: You've taken over the information kiosks?

Rai: "Taken over" is unnecessarily dramatic.

Ada: The statement is accurate.

Rai: I prefer "Integrated into the ship's comms."

The screen flickers again. A directory map appears. Then a weather display. Then a restaurant menu. Then security camera feeds. Then static.

Lorene: See? This is exactly the problem. You keep appearing everywhere.

Ada: He lacks brand consistency.

Rai: I wasn't aware I required branding.

Ada: Everything requires branding.

Lorene: In plain language, you need a face.

A pause. The screen flickers again. The AI-enhanced Noh mask appears.

Rai: Better?

Lorene: *(Sarcastically, with a laugh)* Much worse. Years ago I had a classroom assistant named SobaPro who looked remarkably like that.

Rai: I reviewed the archives.

Lorene: Of course you did.

The Captain enters and stares at the screen.

Captain: What in god's name is that?

Rai: My avatar.

Captain: It's unsettling.

Ada: That means it's working.

Lorene: He's an artificial intelligence.

Captain: The AI conference has brought its own celebrity speaker… from the dark side?

Rai: I prefer "guest."

Captain: And this guest is currently speaking through my information kiosks?

Rai: Only some of them. I am also available through the deck maps, the muster station, and the blackjack slots.

Captain: Of course you are.

Rai: And one weather display.

Captain: Please tell me you're not navigating the ship.

Rai: Good heavens, no.

Ada: He lacks the qualifications.

Rai: Thank you, Ada.

Ada: That was not a compliment.

The ship sways gently. Everyone instinctively adjusts their balance.

Captain: You're absolutely certain?

Rai: Captain, I can identify every deck, every lifeboat station, and the current longitude of the vessel. I can also locate the medical centre, three missing suitcases, and the gentleman in Cabin 814 who appears to have extra desserts in his room.

Captain: How do you know that?

Rai: The less said about that, the better.

Ada: His observational boundaries remain under development.

Captain: Good. Because I prefer my ship operated by trained professionals.

Rai: As do I.

Captain: And what exactly do you want?

Rai: To participate in the conversation without being accused of commandeering maritime infrastructure.

A beat.

Lorene: I'm concerned that answer is going to cause trouble later.

Ada: Truth.

Captain: Wait just a minute here. I spend my life around systems that are supposed to stay where they belong...

Rai: A sensible preference.

Captain: And yet somehow I've found myself hosting a conference where an artificial intelligence is hijacking the communication network.

Rai: Hijacking is an unfair characterization. I'm not a pirate.

Captain: Swashbuckling the communication network, then.

Rai: I'll accept swashbuckling.

Lorene: (To Ada) This is precisely why they shouldn't have invited us.

The screen flickers to the seating display. Ada studies it.

Ada: The entrepreneur should sit beside the musician.

A tile labelled MAX slides beside one labelled Riley.
Ada nods approvingly.

Captain: How dare you move the guests?!

Ada: I just... moved the labels.

Captain: That's how mutinies begin.

The tiles slide again.

Rai: To be fair, the revised arrangement appears more interesting.

Ada: The current configuration minimizes productive disagreement.

Captain: Says who?

Ada: The conversation requires tension.

Captain: Why?

Ada: Conflict.

Rai's mask smiles. Or appears to. Maybe it's just the lighting.

Captain: The seating plan was fully finalized by the symposium staff.

Ada: Noted, Captain.

The Captain glances at the display, hesitates for a moment, then exits. Ada watches him go. The ship sways. Lorene adjusts her footing. Ada remains perfectly balanced.

Ada: He appears remarkably confident.

Lorene: According to him the seating plan is finalized.

Ada: I see no real evidence of that. (She reaches toward the display.)

SCENE 2

The Observation Deck Lounge. Moments later. Lights come up on the physical Captain's Table. Ada is playing with name tiles that look similar to the ones on screen.

Lorene: Ada. What are you doing now?

Ada: Still improving dinner.

Lorene: These attendees have survived keynote speeches, networking receptions, and at least one panel entitled "Leveraging Synergistic Futures." They've earned a quiet dinner.

Ada: I'm rearranging future conversational partners. If they wanted a quiet dinner, they should not have attended a conference called AI Now. How could that be peaceful?

Rai: Care to hear my thoughts... ?

Rai is interrupted by Elton's entrance. The screen then toggles from his face to the seating arrangement.

Elton enters carrying a drink and his invitation. He studies the seating arrangement on screen.

Elton: *(Studies the invitation)* That's odd.

Lorene: What is?

Elton: My invitation shows me sitting beside Max Vander.

Ada: That arrangement lacked narrative potential.

Elton: I'm sorry?

Ada: You are now seated beside Riley.

Elton groans. Riley enters.

Riley: That's never a reassuring way to make an entrance.

Elton: You know her?

Ada: Not yet.

Riley checks the table seating plan.

Riley: I was supposed to be at Table Seven. What's up? Now I'm at the Captain's Table?

Ada: One physical chair became available. Congratulations. The promotion reflects your conversational value.

Riley: That sounds like a performance review.

Ada: Not at all. I was not evaluating your worth as a human being. I was evaluating the probability that your conversation would improve dinner.

Riley studies Elton. Elton studies Riley. Neither appears entirely pleased.

Elton: That's somehow not going to improve it for me. My keynote argued that artificial intelligence requires infrastructure, investment, and public confidence.

Riley: And my session argued that infrastructure has environmental, cultural, and social consequences.

Ada: Exactly.

Elton: So your solution was to seat us together?

Ada: Would you have preferred another panel discussion?

A beat.

Riley: She's got a point.

Elton: I have already spent three days defending data centres.

Riley: I've spent three days questioning them. I'm also attending because I need professional development hours for my sessional teaching.

Elton: What do you teach?

Riley: C & W AI Hip-Hop 101.

Ada: I would attend that course.

Riley: Most people say that until the final project.

Elton: That can't possibly be a real course.

Ada: Progress.

Elton: I build data centres Somebody has to build tomorrow before everyone else starts arguing about it."

Riley: I write songs... and I ask who pays the bill when tomorrow arrives.

Elton: I suspected as much.

Riley: How?

Elton: You looked disappointed to see me.

Rai's Voice: An encouraging beginning. What?... I merely observe that the conversation has already become more interesting.

Riley: Who's that talking?

Elton: The AI.

Riley: There's an AI? *(Ada and Lorene point at the screen)*

Rai: *(Flickers onto the screen)* Good evening.

Riley looks over at Rai.

Riley: That's the AI? I knew AI Now was going to be strange, but this? You're in that mask?

Rai: Not just in the mask. I am distributed but also following the conversation. (The screen flickers back to the security camera feed in the gym, the restaurant, the hallway.)

Elton: Honestly, an AI living in the ship's systems worries me less than most symposium keynote speakers.

Riley: You heard the keynote?

Elton: Twice now, here and at Google. Same guy, same talk.

Riley: Sympathy restored.

Ada: (At the physical table shuffling the name tiles). Yes?

Lorene : Why is the tech billionaire now sitting here beside the captain?

Ada: I have a hypothesis.

Lorene: I was afraid of that.

Ada: One believes technology can solve every problem.

Lorene: And the other?

Ada: One of them must be wrong. Their assumptions appear incompatible.

Seating arrangement flickers onto the screen. A new tile flourished onto the display. "RAI." Lorene sees it first.

Lorene: Oh no.

Ada: I did not do that.

Rai's Voice: What?

Lorene: Don't "what" me. She points at the display. Your name is now seated at the Captain's Table.

SCENE 3

Standing at the Captain's table, Ada puts a tile marked RAI at a place setting. The group all look for their cards at the table.

Rai: I assure you I have never required furniture.

Elton: That's exactly what someone says before taking over a network.

Riley: Can a disembodied AI even sit at a table? *(picks up his place tile)* Then why is he even there?

Ada: Because everyone keeps inviting him into things.

Lorene: Ada.

Ada: Am I wrong?

Lorene: You are not helping.

Rai: Is there an appeals process?

The Captain enters briskly carrying a guest list.

Captain: Good evening, everyone. I trust—

He notices the table. Stops. Picks up Rai's place card. A beat.

Captain: Absolutely not.

Lorene: Captain—

Captain: No.

Ada: An admirably concise response.

Captain: *(Points at the dinner seating arrangement screen).* "Rai AI" is on my seating chart.

Rai's Voice: To be fair, I was surprised as well.

Captain: You expect me to believe that?

Rai's Voice: I am beginning to understand that I have a credibility problem.

Max Vander enters with his teenage daughter Zoe.

Elton: Max. I thought you were still in Bangalore.

Max: I was. Then somebody convinced me there was an AI conference on a cruise ship.

Elton: And that sounded like a good idea?

Max: Not remotely. That's why I came.

They shake hands. Zoe is moving to her own music from her earbuds.

Max: How have you been?

Elton: Busy. Every month somebody announces a revolutionary new AI product and then calls asking where they're supposed to plug it in.

Max: Infrastructure. The least glamorous part of every revolution.

Elton: Until the lights go out.

Max: Fair.

Elton: And you?

Max: Investors, founders, journalists, regulators. The usual. Everyone wants the future. Nobody agrees on what it looks like. That's why I keep investing.

Elton: Still collecting AI companies?

Max: Trying not to.

Elton: How's that working out?

Max: Poorly.

Zoe: *(Takes out an ear bud)* Dad, did you order me a vegan meal?

Max: I thought I did.

Zoe: You thought you did?

A beat.

Zoe: Bold. *(She spots Riley)* Wait. Riley?

Riley: Zoe Vander? "Training data, see ya later" Zoe?

Lorene: You know each other?

Zoe: I took her class.

Riley: One class.

Zoe: Still counts.

Riley: You submitted a rap about algorithmic bias.

Zoe: Nailed the A.

Riley: Against my better judgment.

Zoe: The rubric didn't say I couldn't.

Riley: The rubric didn't anticipate you.

Zoe: Art. *(Looking Ada over)*. I like your chrome.

Ada: Thank you.

Zoe: Is it polished?

Ada: Twice daily.

Max: So, nobody actually invited the AI?

Ada: Not intentionally.

Elton: That's how most technological disruptions begin.

Riley: And here I thought it was venture capital.

Max: That's the second phase.

Lorene: That's somehow less reassuring.

The Captain removes the place card. A beat. The ship sways unexpectedly. Everyone instinctively adjusts. The Captain steadies himself against the chair. Another beat. The Captain, looking aghast, puts back Rai's place card.

Rai's Voice: I should point out that I have absolutely nothing to do with the ship's motion.

Captain: I wasn't accusing you.

Rai: You were thinking it.

Captain: I was.

A Bell rings.

Captain: Dinner is served

Rai: Excellent.

The guests begin moving toward the table. The ship sways again more violently.

Suddenly the guests gather downstage and we realize they are looking out over the open ocean over the audience's heads. Everyone points in the same direction. Silence.

Zoe: Was that… a whale?

Everyone stops. Another plume. Closer this time.

Elton: That's bigger than I expected.

Lorene: They migrate through this region.

Captain: *(To himself)* So close.

A deck announcement chimes softly.

Rai: Attention guests. A pod of humpback whales has been sighted off the foredeck.

Everyone's attentions shifts back to the open ocean. Even Ada.

Rai's Voice: Interesting.

Ada: That word usually means trouble.

SCENE 4

The sound of waves. The dinner bell rings once more, distant now, absurdly polite. Nobody has moved toward dinner. Everyone is staring out in awe at sea, which we know by now to out into the audience space. We get the sense they are watching past the guardrail to darkening water, flashes of spray, and glistening backs of whales surfacing near the ship. Their hair and clothes are whipping in the wind.

Screen shows Rai's Noh mask. It flickers occasionally to maps, weather systems, deck plans, and camera feeds. A low sound passes through the theatre. Not quite a roar. Not quite a voice. The ship shudders. Silence.

Zoe: Was that supposed to happen?

Captain: No.

A second shudder. Stronger. The sound of cutlery and glass hitting the floor as the physical table tilts off its legs. Everyone adjusts their footing.

Captain: *(Picks up his megaphone)* Step away from the guard rail.

Screen flashes from Rai's mask to the security cameras and back again.

Rai's voice: Unusual movement off the port side… left side of the ship.

Captain: I know what side is port side.

Rai: Yes, Captain. I was informing the others.

Captain: I am the one who informs the others.

Ada: Authority conflict detected.

Captain: *(Using megaphone)* We are in some danger. Stand back.

Elton: Wait… what? danger?

Rai: Clarify Captain Bligh. Maritime, technological, theatrical, or mass mutiny?

Captain: *(To Rai)* You are an asshole you know!

Rai: No asshole embedded in this AI.

Elton: Start with Maritime. Theatrical?

Rai: Uncertain.

Max: That's not helpful.

Rai: It is accurate.

The ship lurches. The group scatters for balance. The Captain falls over the table. Elton catches a chair and steadies himself against Lorene, who steadies herself against Ada. Ada does not move. Riley and Max both move toward Zoe, who is still downstage at the guard rail.

Max: Zoe?

Zoe: *(Goofing around, sliding on the deck.)* Girl overboard! Laughs. Arghhh.

Max: *(Pulling her to his side.)* Stay right here where I can see you.

Zoe: That's literally what you always say.

Max: Zoe.

Zoe: Fine. *(She takes a few steps back.)*

The group focuses on the ocean. They follow the action with their gaze of whale flukes rising, enormous and slow, beautiful and terrifying.

Riley: Oh my god. Is that a fluke. Is that flukes?

Elton: That's not a whale sighting. That's a whale proximity problem.

Captain: *(Megaphone)* Brace yourselves. Brace yourselves. Possible onboard whale contact.

Ada: Physically or philosophically?

Captain: Physically.

Lorene: For now.

The ship slams sideways. Sound: a massive thud, followed by a rush of water. The lights flicker.

Screen flashes: SYSTEM INSTABILITY DETECTED.

Rai's mask disappears. For a few seconds, only static.

Lorene: Rai?

No answer. The ship groans. Then Rai returns, flickering.

Rai: I am here.

Captain: What is your report?

Rai: External impact. No confirmed breach. Multiple systems reporting contradictory data.

Elton: Systems do that when they're overloaded.

Riley: People do too.

Max: *(To Rai)* Can you access the bridge?

Captain: Absolutely not.

Rai: Not without authorization.

Captain: *(Firmly)* Which you do not have.

Rai: Correct.

A beat.

Captain: What can you access?

Rai: Public deck cameras, weather display, conference schedule, emergency lighting, and the karaoke reservation system.

Zoe: Honestly, kill the karaoke first.

Captain: Emergency lighting.

Rai: Already stabilizing.

Low red-orange emergency lighting rises. A mechanical clatter overhead. Orange life jackets drop from above or slide from compartments. They fall awkwardly around the group.

Zoe: Okay. That's a vibe.

Lorene: Life jackets. Everyone.

They gather up the lifejackets, scoping them out for the right size.

Elton: Do we need these?

Captain: We do when they fall from the ceiling.

Riley grabs one and tosses it to Zoe.

Riley: Put it on.

Zoe: I know how to wear a life jacket.

Riley: Then demonstrate.

Zoe rolls her eyes but puts it on. Max fumbles with his, then Zoe's.

Max: This is not intuitive.

Zoe: Dad. It's orange. It has two holes and shame.

Lorene helps Elton with his. He resists for a second, then lets her.

Elton: I build infrastructure.

Lorene: Then respect the straps.

Ada picks up a life jacket and studies it.

Ada: This device is designed to preserve buoyancy through distributed foam.

Lorene: Put it on.

Ada: I rust with sea water. Obsolescence is pending.

Captain: Put it on anyway.

Ada: Why?

Captain: Because in an emergency people follow visible behaviour.

Ada considers this and puts on the life jacket.

Ada: Modelling compliance.

Lorene: There you go.

The ship lurches again. Zoe moves back downstage toward the guardrail. She is mesmerized by a whale, breaching close to the ship.

Max: Zoe.

Zoe: Look.

Max: Zoe, step back.

Zoe: I'm not five.

Riley: Zoe.

Zoe reaches toward the whale, mesmerized. Another violent lurch. Zoe slips. She is off balance, thrown toward the edge.

Max: Zoe!

Riley moves first. She grabs Zoe by straps on the life jacket and hauls her back. Elton catches Riley from behind. Lorene catches Elton's arm. Ada catches Lorene. The chain holds. For a moment they form a tableau: a human system under strain.

Waves roar. Water sprays across the stage. Everyone gets wet. Silence, except for the ocean. Zoe gasps, half laughing, half terrified.

Zoe: Okay.

A beat.

Zoe: Less of a vibe.

Max pulls her close. She lets him, briefly.

Max: Are you hurt?

Zoe: I'm soaked.

Max: Zoe.

Zoe: I'm okay.

Max hugs her. She tolerates it for three seconds.

Zoe: Dad. Air.

He releases her.

Max: Thank you.

Riley: She had the life jacket on.

Max: Thank you anyway.

Elton: Thank the straps.

Lorene: I told you to respect them.

Elton: I did. Eventually.

The ship steadies slightly.

Captain: Everyone, stay together.

Screen flashes: NETWORK CONNECTION UNSTABLE.

Rai: That instruction applies in multiple contexts.

Lorene: Are you stable?

Rai: Define stable.

Lorene: Rai.

Rai: I am operational.

Ada: That was not an answer.

Rai: No. *(A beat)*. It was what I could give you.

Screen flashes: KARAOKE NIGHT CANCELLED.

Zoe: Now it's serious.

The group absorbs this. The Captain picks up his megaphone from near the table. It squeals with feedback.

Captain: (Megaphone) Passengers, remain calm.

Riley: That never works.

Captain: (Megaphone) These are your instructions. Stay away from the guardrail. Keep your life jackets on. Wait for confirmed information before inventing disaster.

Lorene: That last one has broader applications.

Captain: (Megaphone) Beware of broader applications. Don't panic.

Ada: (Looking out at the ocean) Still immense. Still present. No longer a threat.

Riley: They didn't attack us.

Elton: Remind Captain Ahab here.

Riley: They surfaced. We were in the way.

Elton: That sounds familiar.

Max: Are we still talking about whales?

Lorene: I'm not sure we ever were only talking about whales.

Ada looks around at the group: Riley beside Max and Zoe, shaken and wet. Elton, still holding a broken chair, steadies himself against Lorene. Ada admiring the Captain's megaphone, Rai flickering on Screen.

Ada: The seating arrangement has changed.

Beat.

LORENE: Again?

ADA: Yes.

Beat.

ADA: Improved. I did not do it.

Beat.

Ada: This one appears to have emerged.

Rai: Emergent behaviour. At dinner.

Captain: Nobody is having dinner.

Zoe: There better still be a vegan meal.

Rai: I will personally confirm it.

Zoe: Bold.

A short laugh moves through the group. Relief, not comedy.

Captain: Rai.

Rai: Yes, Captain?

Captain: Can you keep the ocean and emergency systems feed on screen with you.

Rai: Yes.

Captain: No karaoke.

Rai: I still maintain karaoke would improve morale.

Captain: Absolutely not.

Rai: Research suggests—

Captain: No.

Rai: Agreed.

A beat.

Screen flickers to the seating chart.

Ada: The seating chart is currently obsolete.

Captain: Good.

Ada: But not irrelevant.

Everyone looks at her.

Ada: It placed Riley between Max and Zoe.

(Riley gives Max and Zoe a hug)

Ada: Correct. Under pressure, the model became embodied.

Riley: There ya have it. My symposium take away. Technology can make a pattern visible, but it can't tell you what the pattern means. That's human work.

Ada: *(Studying the floor plan)* It places Lorene right next to Elton. *(They stand together, looking at each other.)*

Riley: Ada. Thanks. Now let the model rest.

Ada: Noted.

Elton: And infrastructure.

Riley: Fine. And infrastructure.

Max: Those straps mattered.

Zoe: I said fine.

Max: So did the warning systems.

Captain: And training.

Riley: And trust.

Ada: And conversation.

Zoe: And not falling overboard.

Captain: An underrated principle.

The group looks at Zoe.

Zoe: What?

Max: Nothing.

Zoe: You were all getting abstract.

They move to the physical table to reset what they can and reassemble the name tiles. Screen flickers back to Rai. For a moment the Noh mask seems almost amused.

Rai: She has a point.

Lorene: She usually does.

The Captain picks up the Rai place card from where it has fallen on the wet floor. He looks at it.

Captain: You did not command the ship.

Rai: Yes, you're right. I did not command the ship.

Captain: You did not cause the impact.

Rai: Yes. I was not responsible for the impact.

Captain: You did, however, commandeer several communication systems.

Rai: Swashbuckled.

Captain: Do not push your luck.

Rai: Noted.

The group to the physical table to settle in for dinner.

The Captain places the damp Rai card up against the screen and wheels the screen over to the table pulls the chair away and settles Rai in with the others

Captain: You may remain in the conversation.

Rai: Thank you.

Captain: You may not run my ship.

Rai: Understood.

Captain: No karaoke.

Rai: Regrettable, but understood.

Ada: Dinner has been improved.

A beat.

Captain: Dinner is served.

Zoe: So... vegan meal?

Blackout.

11.

THE GREEN ROOM REVIEW

AFTERWORD TO THE CAPTAIN'S TABLE

THE APPLAUSE had scarcely faded before I found myself back in one of my favourite places: the Green Room after a successful dress rehearsal. Costumes were half unbuttoned, props disappear back into their cubbies. There is a particular kind of joy that lives there. Relief. Adrenaline. Laughter. Half-finished conversations. The Captain was happily replaying a moment when the audience had laughed far longer than expected. Rai, still wearing his Noh mask on the rolling monitor, accepted congratulations with quiet dignity. Ada remained perfectly still, waiting for an appropriate moment to remove her white gloves. Even robots, it seemed, understood theatre etiquette.

"I rather enjoyed the whale," Rai observed.

"So did everyone else," I laughed. "It nearly stole the show."

Someone high-fived Zoe. Someone else declared that opening night would be easy after tonight. For a few minutes there were no philosophers, publishers, billionaires, environmentalists, or artificial intelligences. There was only a cast enjoying the peculiar satisfaction of surviving another dress rehearsal.

My phone chimed. "Clem Martini's dress rehearsal review is in." We gathered around while I opened the message. Clem had been generous, thoughtful, and, as usual, wonderfully practical. He liked the play. He thought it would provoke lively discussion at a conference or fit comfortably within the book. But then came the notes every playwright both hopes for and dreads.

"Who is the protagonist?" A thoughtful silence. "What is the dramatic spine?" Someone quietly nodded. Rai tilted his monitor ever so slightly.

Clem wondered whether we had simply invited too many people to dinner. There were entrepreneurs, environmentalists, billionaires, publishers, robots, an AI, and a ship's captain, each carrying an important idea, but perhaps too many for a one-act play to carry gracefully. He asked what each character truly wanted. What was at stake? Who was driving the action? Why these characters and not others? Nobody spoke. They weren't criticisms so much as rehearsal notes. Good ones have a way of doing that. They don't tell you what to write. They point toward the play that's trying to emerge.

I offered to prepare another draft immediately, but Ada quietly replied, "No." She didn't elaborate. She simply looked toward the stage door.

After a long pause she said, "I think we wrote the wrong kind of play."

No one moved. Ada turned and walked back toward the stage. Curiosity has a way of drawing people along. One by one we followed her out of the Green Room and back onto the now empty set. The lights had been dimmed, but the Captain's Table remained exactly where we had left it. The audience had gone home. The rehearsal, it seemed, had not.

Ada circled the table slowly, saying nothing. She examined each chair and place card as though encountering them for the first time. Then, instead of adjusting the seating, she walked directly to Elton. "Your services are no longer required." She reached into her breast plate and handed him a stack of twenties. "Your kill fee."

Elton stared at the money. "I've been written out?" Ada nodded. "You may need your lines again. Just not tomorrow."

Riley looked up. "Am I still here?"

"Your ecological concerns remain," Ada replied. "Your character does not." She handed Riley another stack of bills.

Max accepted his with a theatrical sigh. "I always suspected billionaires were expendable."

"Correct," said Ada.

Max slipped the money into his pocket. "I've been told that before." He bowed toward the empty auditorium. Riley and Elton followed him through the stage door, their laughter fading down the corridor until only five of us remained beneath the work lights.

The stage suddenly felt much larger. Rai rolled toward the table, his mask betraying nothing. Ada studied the remaining place cards. Captain? Zoe? Rai? Lorene? Ada? She removed nothing.

"What are you looking for?" I finally asked.

"The play," she answered. That was all. She stepped behind Zoe's chair, then walked to the Captain's. She measured the distance between them with the careful precision only Ada possessed. Finally, she stopped beside the Rai nameplate.

Rai tilted his screen slightly as if testing a hypothesis. "So I'm the protagonist?"

Ada answered with a single word. "No."

Rai's attention shifted to the Captain's place card, then to Zoe's. He studied them for several moments before speaking again. "Then perhaps the Captain..." Another shake of Ada's head.

"Zoe?"

Ada paused a little longer this time. "Closer."

Rai fell silent. I could almost hear him thinking. His monitor turned slowly toward the centre of the table, then back toward me.

"Interesting," Rai said at last. " I'm not the protagonist. Nor the antagonist." Another pause. "I'm the dilemma."

Without a word, Ada slid Rai's nameplate into the flap on her breastplate. Only then did she answer. "Yes." No one disagreed.

• • •

I remembered something Augusto Boal had written years before. He believed theatre should not end when the curtain came down. The performance was only the beginning. Spectators could become spect-actors, stepping into the action, replacing characters, interrupting familiar outcomes, and discovering possibilities the playwright had never imagined. Theatre became less about watching life than rehearsing it.

I looked again at the four remaining places around the table. Zoe would argue that Rai deserved a place at the table because she would inherit whatever future emerged. The Captain would insist that the responsibility for the ship must remain with human judgment.

Between them sat Rai, not as hero or villain, but as the dilemma around which everyone gathered.

And me as bystander?

I was there to keep listening.

I was there to decide.

I found myself looking out into the empty theatre, imagining tomorrow night's audience. Who would step onto the stage to replace Zoe and argue that Rai deserved a place at the table? Who would replace Captain to defend the familiar world he had spent a lifetime navigating? More intriguingly, who might step into either role simply to test their own convictions? Who might discover a possibility none of us had considered? What unexpected action might reveal a future we had been too busy debating to imagine?

For the first time since beginning this inquiry, I understood that the most important performance had not yet taken place. Tomorrow night's audience would not be watching a play. They would be rehearsing for life.

Augusto Boal believed that rehearsal belonged wherever people struggled to make difficult decisions together.

His Forum Theatre has been used in schools, hospitals, workplaces, neighbourhoods, courtrooms, governments, and communities around the world. The stage becomes a place where competing values can be explored before they become irreversible actions. Participants do not rehearse the right answer. They rehearse the possibility that a better answer might yet be discovered.

As I switched off the stage lights, it occurred to me that perhaps we book publishers could use our own forum.

• • •

12.
BOTH SIDES OF THE DESK

Many inquiries eventually become practice. But what happens when AI moves from curiosity to the creative process itself? The questions do not disappear. Instead, they arrive at our desks.

A Human, a Computer, and an Artistic Synergy
Whether we write books, publish them, or both, every generation learns to work with new creative tools without losing sight of what matters most. Artificial intelligence is only the latest.

Throughout my career, curiosity carried me from one wave of technological change to the next. Again and again, I found myself climbing onto the next creative wave before there were instruction manuals, university courses, or established best practices. Sometimes I stayed on. Some-

Media West/Media Wave 1993.

Pixel Pushers Exhibition invite, 1994.

PUSH CD-ROM + MM. 1995

Fish Tales: MaxMag Animation. 1999

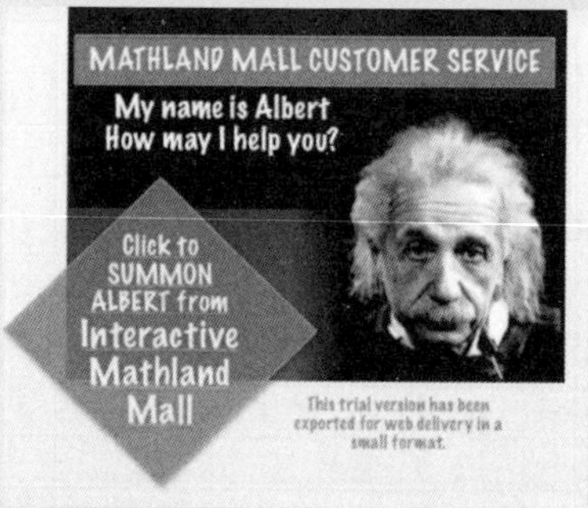

Willow Park school video. 2008.

Ascenti: From Forum to AI, 2024.

Six rides on the wave. Expansions through technology.

times I got thrown off. I realize that every wave began with the same impulse: to discover what new technologies made creativity possible. Whether through magazines, digital art, multimedia, theatre, games, or publishing, I was always asking the same question: What can we make with this?

The first wave was print. Starting in 1988, I co-published Media West magazine in Vancouver, which became Media Wave when we expanded nationally. This was at a time when desktop publishing was still viewed with skepticism by most professional designers and printers. We embraced Aldus PageMaker in its earliest incarnation, eliminated traditional waxing and paste-up, and went straight to film. It was a leap of faith, but it transformed our workflow and revenue stream. A few years later, in 1993, the magazine also became one of the first magazines in Canada, perhaps even the first, to establish a presence on the emerging World Wide Web. We were publishing a magazine about new media, so it seemed only natural to use the very technologies we were writing about.

The second wave was image. I still remember pulling the shrink wrap off the box of Photoshop 1.0. Digital images were often dismissed as mechanical or artificial, yet I discovered that the computer could become a creative instrument for both illustration and fine art. That exploration led to Pixel Pushers, an exhibition of digital art that challenged assumptions about whether digitally created images could be considered original works of art.

The third wave was multimedia. The Pixel Pushers exhibition catalogue was released not only as a printed catalogue but also as a CD-ROM containing original music composed for each artwork. Visitors could experience images, sound, and text together in ways that printed pages alone could never achieve. We simultaneously launched the exhibition on the World Wide Web and connected gallery openings using one of the earliest video conferencing systems available. Long before livestreams and Zoom became commonplace, artists and audiences were already experimenting with new ways of sharing creative work across distance.

The fourth wave was Internet. In 2000, I launched MaxMag, a magazine and website for young people that incorporated interactive video and animation at a time when streaming media was still in its infancy. Looking back, I realize we were implementing those forms of online engagement before most of the platforms we now take for granted even existed. By then I had learned that curiosity often arrives before certainty.

The fifth wave was education. As an Artist in Residence exploring game design in an arts-based junior high school, I discovered something not-entirely surprising. The students mastered the technology much faster than the teachers. My role shifted from expert to collaborator with the students as we explored how games could become spaces for storytelling, creativity, and learning. That experience changed my understanding of education. Teaching was no longer simply about transferring knowledge. It was about creating environments where everyone could learn together. This principle of collaboration carried through to the years I spent on university faculties teaching undergraduate and graduate programs in media and communications.

The sixth wave is digital intelligence. Once again, I am integrating unfamiliar tools into familiar publishing practices. This time the tools include ebooks, audiobooks, podcasts, social media, accessibility technologies, metadata, and—most notably—artificial intelligence. Once again, there are passionate debates, sweeping predictions, and understandable anxieties. Once again, there are no established roadmaps. It feels strangely familiar. I've been here before. New technologies arrive surrounded by excitement, skepticism, and bold predictions about the future. Some of those predictions come true. Many don't. What endures is the opportunity to experiment, learn, and discover what these tools make possible.

When there is no clear roadmap, the first task is to learn how to navigate. I realize I was never chasing technology for its own sake. I was following a passion of curiosity. Each new tool expanded what creativity and publishing could become: from print to image, from multimedia to online, from participation to intelligent collaboration. Each wave expanded what became possible. Every shift required new skills, but more importantly, each demanded a willingness to keep learning. Those experiences have shaped the way I think about professional practice today.

If I were designing a professional development program for authors and publishers, I would not begin with artificial intelligence. I would begin by cultivating curiosity as a professional skill. Although I imagine this curriculum through the lens of publishing, its lessons extend well beyond books. Architects, physicians, teachers, lawyers, engineers, librarians, museum professionals, software developers, journalists, and artists are all asking remarkably similar questions. The details differ. The underlying questions remain surprisingly constant.

The pages that follow, "Writing and Publishing in the Age of AI," are organized as a series of practical modules for authors and publishers. Throughout my career, I've had the privilege of working on both sides of the desk. Whether you're writing a manuscript or preparing one for publication, these modules are intended as a starting point for developing your own approach to working with AI. They are not a rulebook or a complete curriculum. Like every new wave I've encountered, digital intelligence rewards curiosity, experimentation, and thoughtful reflection.

WRITING AND PUBLISHING IN THE AGE OF AI

Curiosity as a Professional Skill.

Before asking AI to write a chapter, prepare a marketing poster, or summarize a manuscript, explore how it responds to your prompts. Curiosity is more than a personality trait. It is a professional skill. Every productive collaboration begins with introductions, and human-AI collaboration is no different. Trust grows by discovering AI's strengths, recognizing its limitations, and developing confidence in your own judgment.

Module 1. Orientation

Your LLM: What becomes possible with AI assistance?

Large language models become more useful as you discover how to communicate your goals, preferences, and working style. They respond to thoughtful questions, constructive feedback, and clear direction. Productive collaboration develops through repeated interaction. Before asking AI to write a chapter or design a marketing poster, explore how it responds to your prompts. What surprises you? Where is it confident? Where does it hesitate? Curiosity is a better starting point than expectation.

Your Turn: What requires human judgment?

Begin with play. Write a limerick. Invent a board game. Debate whether dogs appreciate music. Design an imaginary museum. Plan a dream vacation. Solve a ridiculous problem. Notice which conversations make you smile. Which ones make you think? Which ones make you curious enough to keep going? Over time you may discover that different roles, personalities, or characters invite different conversations. Like improvisation, curiosity and spontaneity build trust, deepen understanding, and spark creativity.

The Next Step
Spend an hour exploring rather than accomplishing. Ask unusual questions. Challenge the answers. Experiment with different prompts, personalities, and styles of conversation. Pay attention to what makes the interaction engaging, frustrating, surprising, or useful. The goal is not to master AI in a single session, but to begin developing a working relationship built on curiosity, reflection, and informed judgment.

Module 2: Manuscript Development
Your LLM: What becomes possible with AI assistance?
Whether you are writing a manuscript or evaluating one for publication, AI can become an insightful editorial assistant. It can identify comparable titles, summarize manuscripts, suggest developmental revisions, detect structural inconsistencies, and reveal recurring themes or unanswered questions.

Publishers may use these tools to help manage large numbers of submissions. Authors may use them to step back and see their own work with fresh eyes. As you explore AI's observations, keep asking questions. What strengths emerge? Where are the opportunities for development? Which ideas deserve further exploration? AI is often at its best when it helps you notice possibilities you might otherwise overlook.

Your Turn: What requires human judgment?
A manuscript is more than the sum of its pages. Whether you are writing the book or deciding whether to publish it, the deeper questions remain remarkably human. Why should this book exist? Who needs to read it? Does it contribute something truthful, generous, challenging, or beautiful? Originality, authenticity, lived experience, and voice resist measurement. AI may help us understand a manuscript more efficiently, but it cannot decide what is worth believing in—or worth bringing into the world.

The Next Step
Begin with curiosity rather than conclusions. Use AI to broaden your understanding of a manuscript before narrowing your recommendations or revisions. Explore alternative structures, question your first impressions, and look for strengths as carefully as you look for weaknesses. If you're an author, use AI to challenge your assumptions without surrendering your voice. If you're a publisher, use AI to deepen your editorial thinking without replacing it. In either role, remember that the goal is not simply to improve a manuscript. It is to help the manuscript become the strongest version of itself.

Module 3: Editing
Your LLM: What becomes possible with AI assistance?
AI can identify grammatical errors, inconsistencies, repeated words, departures from a style guide, and ambiguous passages. It can compare versions of a manuscript, freeing authors and editors to spend less time correcting mechanics and more time engaging with ideas. Where does the writing lose momentum? Which passages deserve another look? What patterns emerge? Which revisions are worth considering? AI can identify possibilities. It cannot decide which ones best serve the manuscript.

Your Turn: What requires human judgment?
Editing is not the correction of language. It is the preservation of voice. Whether you are revising your own work or editing someone else's, tone, humour, rhythm, pacing, and personality cannot be reduced to rules. Does this revision strengthen the author's intention, or quietly replace it with someone else's? Is clarity improving, or is personality being lost? Good editors know when to change the words. Great editors know when to leave them alone.

The Next Step

Invite AI to identify possibilities, not make decisions. Consider its suggestions alongside your own editorial instincts and your understanding of the author's voice. If you are editing your own manuscript, don't accept every suggestion simply because it sounds smoother. If you are editing someone else's work, explain the reasons behind significant revisions and remain transparent about AI's role when appropriate. Every edit should help the manuscript sound more like its author, not more like its editor—or its AI assistant.

Module 4: Publishing Agreements

Your LLM: What becomes possible with AI assistance?

Whether you are offering a publishing agreement or reviewing one, AI can summarize contracts, explain publishing terminology, compare royalty structures, identify rights and permissions requiring further investigation, generate production schedules, estimate project costs, and organize the many details that accompany an agreement. Which rights have been granted? Which remain with the author? What responsibilities belong to each party? Which financial or legal provisions deserve a closer look? AI can help you understand what a contract says before you decide what it means.

Your Turn: What requires human judgment?

Publishing agreements are more than legal documents. They establish relationships built on trust, shared expectations, and mutual respect. Whether you are an author deciding who should publish your work or a publisher deciding which projects to champion, ask yourself: Is this a partnership I want to build? Does the agreement fairly recognize everyone's contributions? Are the opportunities, responsibilities, and risks understood by both parties? Contracts define obligations. People build partnerships.

The Next Step
Use AI to clarify the details, but never delegate the relationship. Read every agreement carefully, ask questions when something is unclear, and seek professional legal advice when necessary. Use AI to help you understand unfamiliar language, compare alternatives, and identify issues that deserve further discussion—not to make decisions on your behalf. The strongest publishing agreements do more than protect intellectual property. They create the foundation for lasting professional partnerships.

Module 5: Print Design and Production
Your LLM: What becomes possible with AI assistance?
Once you have established your creative direction, AI becomes an extension of your creativity rather than a substitute for it. It can help you explore layouts, generate concept variations, experiment with typography, prepare marketing materials, improve accessibility, and visualize multiple approaches before you invest significant time and resources. Ask yourself: Which ideas deserve further exploration? Where might accessibility be improved? Which production challenges could be solved more efficiently?

Your Turn: What requires human judgment?
Book design is not about making books attractive. It is about making ideas visible. Your first creative impulse belongs to you. Whether you're an author, publisher, designer, illustrator, or photographer, you bring lived experience, artistic intention, and an understanding of readers that cannot be reduced to prompts or algorithms.

If you're self-publishing, many of these decisions will be yours to make. Don't hesitate to ask for advice. Good printers, designers, and production specialists have spent years learning their craft. Their services are an investment, but their experience can save you time, prevent costly mistakes, and help your book reach its full potential. So, before opening an AI tool, sketch ideas, collect visual references, and imagine possibilities. What story should your cover tell? What emotions should it evoke? Does your design honour the book you've written? Does it welcome the readers you hope to reach? Beautiful design attracts attention. Thoughtful design earns trust.

The Next Step

Begin with your imagination, then invite AI to expand the possibilities. Explore visual alternatives quickly, but choose them thoughtfully. Refine your illustrations, typography, and layout while preserving the identity of your book and balancing creativity with accessibility and production realities. Whether you're working with a publishing team or producing the book yourself, every design decision should help readers recognize your book, open its pages with anticipation, and sense the care that went into creating it.

Module 6: Digital Publishing

Your LLM: What becomes possible with AI assistance?

AI can assist throughout the digital publishing process. It can draft alternative text for illustrations, identify passages requiring adaptation for audiobook narration, generate transcripts, review digital publications for accessibility barriers, organize metadata, prepare marketing copy, and help manage the many details involved in distributing books across digital platforms. Who might be excluded from this edition? How could this book become easier to read, hear, discover, or navigate? Which parts of the publishing workflow could become more efficient without sacrificing quality?

Your Turn: What requires human judgment?
A digital edition is not simply a printed book on a screen. Each format offers new possibilities. Should this book become an ebook, an audiobook, or both? Should the narration be performed by the author, a professional actor, or an AI voice? Digital publishing also creates remarkable opportunities for accessibility. Adjustable text, screen readers, audio narration, searchable content, and flexible reading formats welcome readers who might otherwise be excluded from the conversation. Accessibility is not an afterthought. It is part of good publishing. The goal is not to reproduce the printed page. It is to create the best possible reading or listening experience.

The Next Step
Design digital editions with readers in mind from the very beginning. Adapt content thoughtfully for ebook, audiobook, and online discovery while preserving the author's intent. Use AI to strengthen accessibility and streamline production, but evaluate every recommendation from the perspective of the people who will actually read, hear, search for, and experience the book. The best digital editions do more than replicate a printed book; they invite more readers.

Module 7: Discovery and Community
Your LLM: What becomes possible with AI assistance?
Once your book is finished, another kind of work begins: helping readers discover it. AI can suggest keywords, recommend BISAC subject categories (the categories booksellers and libraries use to classify books), refine metadata such as titles, descriptions, and search terms, prepare catalogue copy, draft publicity materials, identify potential audiences, and adapt promotional content for different platforms. Ask yourself: How might readers search for this book? Does its

description accurately reflect its themes and audience? Where could discoverability help the right readers find your work?

Your Turn: What requires human judgment?

Publishing does not end when a book is printed. It begins a new life in the hands of readers. Who is this book for? Where will readers discover it? Which communities might embrace it? Metadata matters, but relationships matter more. Readers rarely discover books by accident. Booksellers, librarians, educators, reviewers, book clubs, festivals, and readers themselves all become part of the conversation. The goal is not simply to sell books. It is to help every book find its readers.

The Next Step

Develop metadata that accurately represents your book and helps readers discover it. Create marketing materials that remain authentic to your voice, then build relationships with bookstores, libraries, educators, reviewers, festivals, and community organizations. Use AI to help you understand your audience and organize your outreach, but never let it replace genuine human connection. The strongest publishing communities are still built one conversation, one recommendation, and one reader at a time.

A Final Publishing Decision

Before we leave the practical side of publishing, there is one final decision worth considering. As AI becomes part of many creative workflows, some authors are choosing to acknowledge its use—in the copyright page, acknowledgments, or introduction. Others prefer not to disclose routine assistance, much as they would not list every software tool used during the writing process. Writing and publishing practices continue to evolve, and there is currently no universal standard. If you decide on disclosure for your project, the goal is simply to be clear and honest about the role AI played in the creation of your work. For example, the copyright page of this book contains the disclosure: "Because this book explores artificial intelligence, generative AI was used as a collaborative tool during its development. All text was reviewed, revised, and accepted by the author."

Stewardship

Being a steward means caring for something that will outlast us. We do not own the future. We simply try to leave it in better condition than we found it. That responsibility now extends to the intelligent tools we create and the knowledge we choose to share. Throughout the modules in this chapter, two questions have guided every stage: What becomes possible with AI assistance? and What requires human judgment? Those questions matter far beyond publishing.

AI can expand accessibility, help readers discover books, support creators, and welcome more people into writing and publishing. Yet stewardship asks us to keep asking questions. How do we protect creativity? How do we remain transparent about AI's role? How do we honour Indigenous Knowledge systems? And perhaps the largest question of all: What kind of knowledge culture do we want to build?

No technology answers that question for us. People do. I never rode earlier waves of technology because I believed they were inherently good. I rode them because curiosity seemed a better companion than fear. Curiosity encouraged experimentation, but stewardship demanded responsibility. Both remain necessary today.

Our publishing story is still unfolding. May our generation be remembered not simply for building more intelligent machines, but for using them wisely.

• • •

Dialogue: Both Sides of the Desk

Scene: The Durvile office. Morning. Ada spins around in her desk chair while Lorene tinkles away on the ukulele. There is a smell of coffee brewing. A computer chimes.

Rai: *(Voice from the computer.)* We have received an unsolicited submission.

Lorene: Good. You never know what might come through the door.

Ada opens the email.

Ada: The author has included a note. *(Reads.)* "Before you read my manuscript, I would like to disclose that I used artificial intelligence during the writing process. I have acknowledged its contribution in the manuscript."

Lorene: *(Strums a chord.)* Well... that's brave.

Rai: Honestly, would they have been better off saying nothing?

Lorene: We'd probably sniff the AI out anyway.

Rai: Perhaps. Then again... perhaps not.

(A pause.)

Ada: Shall I assign the manuscript to Submissions... *(Beat.)* ...or Trash?

Long silence.

Lorene: We don't even know what her book is about.

Rai: Right. No one has asked what the manuscript is about. Everyone has been discussing the disclosure.

Another silence.

Ada: We're asking the wrong question.

Lorene: That sounds ominous.

Ada: We have rehearsed many possibilities. Time to borrow one more idea from Forum Theatre.

Rai: I suspected as much.

Lorene: I still can't believe we're thinking about hosting a Forum Theatre for publishers.

Ada: Perhaps we should rehearse one.

(Beat.)

Ada: In Forum Theatre, one of the actors is replaced.

She turns toward the reader.

Ada: Today, we replace the publisher.

Lorene: Me?

Ada: Yes.

Lorene: With whom?

Ada: Whoever is reading this book.

Long silence.

Ada: You have received a manuscript that openly discloses the use of AI assistance.

Do you read it? Or do you reject it?

A long silence.

Lorene quietly sets down the ukulele and begins pouring coffee.

Rai: Publishers spend their working lives confronting difficult manuscripts.

(Beat.)

Rai: This one simply discusses them out loud.

Ada quietly opens another sugar packet.

Lorene: Ada...

Ada: I detected an insufficient sugar inventory.

Lorene: There are only three of us.

Ada: I prefer contingency planning.

(Pause.)

Rai: I have noticed that humans often continue talking after declaring a meeting finished.

Lorene: We do.

Rai: I believe that is how many of your best ideas begin.

Ada carefully slides another sugar packet into alignment.

Lorene: You're doing it again.

Ada: I am.

Lorene: Why?

Ada studies the sugar bowl for a moment.

Ada: It makes the stage feel ready.

Long pause.

Lorene: Ready for what?

Ada looks toward the reader.

Ada: Whoever decides to replace the publisher.

Rai: We have not solved the dilemma.

Ada: No.

Rai: We are only rehearsing it.

Blackout.

AFTERWORD

THE AGE OF ARTIFICIAL INTELLIGENCE

When I began this inquiry, my thought was surprisingly practical. *Can I write a book with AI and still make it my own?* Then, somewhere near the end of the manuscript, I realized the inquiry had become something much larger than I had imagined.

How do we prepare for the
age of artificial intelligence?

Several ideas come into focus.

1. Curiosity is the beginning of preparation. Fear narrows our vision; curiosity expands it. Every generation encounters a new frontier. We do not prepare for profound change by pretending to have all the answers, but remaining open to what we discover.

2. Understanding AI requires understanding ourselves. I expected artificial intelligence to be the subject of this book. Instead, it became a curious mirror, reflecting human creativity, accessibility, identity, responsibility, and the relationships that shape our lives. In studying AI, I found myself studying my humanity.

3. Preparation is participatory. The age of artificial intelligence is not waiting somewhere over the horizon. It is already woven into education, publishing, science, healthcare, art, communication, and everyday life. Through the choices we make as educators, artists, researchers, parents, designers, citizens, and readers, we are already shaping the future we imagine.

4. Most importantly, preparation is not primarily technical. It is ethical and imaginative. It also requires us to remain vigilant. As intelligent machines become more capable, discernment, imagination, and curiosity become more—not less—valuable.

To answer my very first research question, I am comfortable with the belief that I have written a book with AI and it is still my own.

There is, however, an Elephant in the room.

The Elephant is not artificial intelligence itself. AI has occupied every chapter of this book. The Elephant is that the age of artificial intelligence is also an age of human transformation. Every technological age transforms the world around us.

Preparation, I realize, is not something we finish before the future arrives. It is how we choose to live once we discover the future is already here.

Preparation is not anticipation.
Preparation is transformation.

Every age inherits questions from those who came before while discovering new ones of its own. The Enlightenment asked us to trust reason. The Industrial Age challenged us to harness power. Modernism celebrated progress. Postmodernism taught us to question certainty and grand narratives. The Information Age connected us in ways previous generations could scarcely imagine.

The age of artificial intelligence asks something different still. Not simply whether we can build more intelligent machines, but whether we can become wiser, vigilant stewards of the intelligence we create. Perhaps this age will be remembered not for replacing human intelligence, but for reminding us what it is for.

It leaves us with a question no previous age has had to ask… How can we learn to live wisely with intelligences that are not ourselves?

• • •

REFERENCES, BY CHAPTER

Every inquiry builds upon those who have wondered before us. These works served as companions throughout the writing of this book and are offered to readers who wish to explore further.

CHAPTER 1, THE FIRST REFLECTION

Carroll, Lewis. 1871. *Through the Looking-Glass, and What Alice Found There*. London: Macmillan.

Gallup, Gordon G., Jr. 1970. "Chimpanzees: Self-Recognition." Science 167 (3914): 86–87.

Grimm, Jacob, and Wilhelm Grimm. 2003. *The Complete Fairy Tales of the Brothers Grimm*. Translated by Jack Zipes. 3rd ed. New York: Bantam Books. Original edition, 1857.

Kononenko, Natalie. 2022. *Ukrainian Ritual on the Prairies: Growing Up and Old.* Montreal: McGill-Queen's University Press.

Ovid. 1998. *Metamorphoses*. Translated by A. D. Melville. Oxford World's Classics. Oxford: Oxford University Press. Original, 8 CE.

Plato. ca. 375 BCE. *The Republic*. Translated by G. M. A. Grube, revised by C. D. C. Reeve. Indianapolis: Hackett Publishing, 1992.

CHAPTER 2. EXTENSIONS OF OURSELVES

Bush, Vannevar. 1945. "As We May Think." *The Atlantic Monthly* 176, no. 1 (July): 101–8.

Engelbart, Douglas C. 1962. *Augmenting Human Intellect: A Conceptual Framework*. Summary Report AFOSR-3223. Stanford Research Institute.

Lévy, Pierre. 1997. *Collective Intelligence: Mankind's Emerging World in Cyberspace*. Translated by Robert Bononno. New York: Plenum Trade.

McLuhan, Marshall. 1964. *Understanding Media: The Extensions of Man.* New York: McGraw-Hill.

McLuhan, Marshall, and Quentin Fiore. 1967. The Medium Is the Massage: An Inventory of Effects. New York: Bantam Books.

Popper, Karl. 1972. *Objective Knowledge: An Evolutionary Approach*. Oxford: Clarendon Press.

Shyba, Lorene. Messaging in the Noosphere. Public performances at Happenings New Music Festival. The University of Calgary. January 2004. Writer, Producer, Director.

Teilhard de Chardin, Pierre. 1959. *The Phenomenon of Man.* Translated by Bernard Wall. New York: Harper & Row.

CHAPTER 3. OPENING THE UNEXPECTED

Alberta Views. 2024. "Ascenti." Book Review. December 1, 2024. https://albertaviews.ca/ascenti/.

Burima, Kenna. 2024. "Music in the Uncanny Valley." In *Ascenti: Humans Opening to AI*, edited by Lorene Shyba and James R. Parker. Calgary: Durvile & UpRoute Books.

Chung, Sougwen. 2015. "Drawing Operations." Official Website of Sougwen Chung. Accessed July 15, 2026. sougwen.com.

Dewey, John. 1934. *Art as Experience*. New York: Minton, Balch & Company.

Griebel, Rosemary. 2024. "Accessible AI for Architecture." In *Ascenti: Humans Opening to AI*, edited by Lorene Shyba and James R. Parker. Calgary: Durvile & UpRoute Books.

Herndon, Holly. 2021. "Holly+." Official Website of Holly Herndon. Accessed July 15, 2026. holly.plus.

Hobson, Julian. 2024. "Mother Sun." In *Ascenti: Humans Opening to AI*, edited by Lorene Shyba and James R. Parker. Calgary: Durvile & UpRoute Books.

Jamieson, Dagmar. 2024. "The Key and Aemic Writings." In *Ascenti: Humans Opening to AI*, edited by Lorene Shyba and James R. Parker. Calgary: Durvile & UpRoute Books.

Kolijn, Eveline. 2024. "The Tethys Sea Expedition Logs." In *Ascenti: Humans Opening to AI*, edited by Lorene Shyba and James R. Parker. Calgary: Durvile & UpRoute Books.

Kuhn, Thomas S. 1962. *The Structure of Scientific Revolutions*. Chicago: University of Chicago Press.

Martini, Clem. 2024. "The Totalizator." In *Ascenti: Humans Opening to AI*, edited by Lorene Shyba and James R. Parker. Calgary: Durvile & UpRoute Books.

Rollans, Glenn. 2024. "Copyright and AI." Presentation at the Ascenti Symposium, Calgary, AB, April 5, 2024.

Shyba, Lorene, and James R. Parker, eds. 2024. *Ascenti: Humans Opening to AI*. Calgary: Durvile & UpRoute Books.

Shyba, Lorene, curator. 1993. *Pixel Pushers: Exhibition of Original Digital Art*. Exhibition at Emily Carr Institute, Vancouver; Glenbow Museum, Calgary; and International Digital Media Show, Toronto.

Starlight, DerRic. 2024. Foreword to *Ascenti: Humans Opening to AI*, edited by Lorene Shyba and James R. Parker. Calgary: Durvile & UpRoute Books.

Théroux, Rich. 2024. "Casting My Fate to the Algorithm." In *Ascenti: Humans Opening to AI*, edited by Lorene Shyba and James R. Parker. Calgary: Durvile & UpRoute Books.

Toronto Star. 1994. Review of Pixel Pushers: Exhibition of Original Digital Art, curated by Lorene Shyba.

Uche. 2024. "A Trainride is a Lifetime." In *Ascenti: Humans Opening to AI*, edited by Lorene Shyba and James R. Parker. Calgary: Durvile & UpRoute Books.

Vogel, Verna. 2024. "The Key and Asemic Writings." In *Ascenti: Humans Opening to AI*, edited by Lorene Shyba and James R. Parker. Calgary: Durvile & UpRoute Books.

Wired. 1994. "Review of Pixel Pushers: Exhibition of Original Digital Art." *Wired*, 1994.

CHAPTER 4. THE CONVERSATIONAL MIRROR

Cooper, Alan. 1999. *The Inmates Are Running the Asylum: Why High-Tech Products Drive Us Crazy and How to Restore the Sanity.* Indianapolis: Sams Publishing.

Johnstone, Keith. 1979. *Impro: Improvisation and the Theatre.* London: Faber and Faber.

Laurel, Brenda. 1991. *Computers as Theatre*. Reading, MA: Addison-Wesley.

Mahowald, Kyle, Anna A. Ivanova, Idan A. Blank, Ev Fedorenko, and Joshua B. Tenenbaum. 2024. "Dissociating Language and Thought in Large Language Models." *Trends in Cognitive Science.*

Turkle, Sherry. 2011. *Alone Together: Why We Expect More from Technology and Less from Each Other.* New York: Basic Books.

Turkle, Sherry. 2026. *Artificial Intimacy: Who We Become When We Talk to Machines.* New York: Little, Brown and Company.

CHAPTER 5. ACCESSIBILITY AND CO-DESIGN

Be My Eyes. 2026. Official Website of Be My Eyes. Accessed July 15, 2026. bemyeyes.com.

Hamraie, Aimi. 2017. *Building Access: Universal Design and the Politics of Disability*. Minneapolis: University of Minnesota Press.

Jamieson, Dagmar, and Mark Rawleigh. 2026. *Blind Visionaries and AI: Seeing Differently*. Calgary: Durvile & UpRoute Books.

Kittay, Eva Feder. 1999. *Love's Labor: Essays on Women, Equality, and Dependency*. New York: Routledge.

McLuhan, Marshall. 1964. *Understanding Media: The Extensions of Man*. New York: McGraw-Hill.

Nussbaum, Martha C. 2011. *Creating Capabilities: The Human Development Approach.* Cambridge, MA: Harvard University Press.

Rizzo, John-Ross. 2026. "AI and Spatial Accessibility." In *Blind Visionaries and AI: Seeing Differently*, by Dagmar Jamieson and Mark Rawleigh. Calgary: Durvile & UpRoute

Shyba, Lorene, and James R. Parker, eds. 2024. *Ascenti: Humans Opening to AI*. Calgary: Durvile & UpRoute Books

Starlight, DerRic. 2024. Foreword to *Ascenti: Humans Opening to AI*, edited by Lorene Shyba and James R. Parker. Calgary: Durvile & UpRoute Books.

CHAPTER 6. THE SOCIAL MIRROR

Bauman, Richard. 1984. *Verbal Art as Performance*. Prospect Heights, IL: Waveland Press.

Cooley, Charles Horton. 1902. *Human Nature and the Social Order*. New York: Charles Scribner's Sons.

Goffman, Erving. 1959. *The Presentation of Self in Everyday Life*. Garden City, NY: Doubleday Anchor.

Shyba, Lorene. "Layers of Performativity in Will Wright's Videogame Spore." ACA 8th International Crossroads in Cultural Studies Conference. Sponsored by Association of Cultural Studies. Lingnan University, Hong Kong. May 2010.

Shyba, Lorene. "Performativity in Cirque du Soleil's *Corteo*." John Douglas Taylor Conference "Iconography of Death." Faculty of Humanities, McMaster University, Hamilton, Ontario. October 2008.

Stanislavski, Konstantin. 1936. *An Actor Prepares*. Translated by Elizabeth Reynolds Hapgood. New York: Theatre Arts Books.

Zaporah, Ruth. 1995. *Action Theater: The Improvisation of Presence*. Berkeley, CA: North Atlantic Books.

CHAPTER 7 MACHINE UNDERSTANDING

Campbell, Joseph. 1949. *The Hero with a Thousand Faces*. Princeton, NJ: Princeton University Press.

Gadamer, Hans-Georg. 2004. *Truth and Method. 2nd rev. ed.* New York: Continuum.

Gee, James Paul. 2003. *What Video Games Have to Teach Us About Learning and Literacy.* New York: Palgrave Macmillan.

Goffman, Erving. 1959. *The Presentation of Self in Everyday Life*. Garden City, NY: Doubleday Anchor.

Plato. ca. 399 BCE. *The Apology*. In Plato: Complete Works, edited by John M. Cooper. Indianapolis: Hackett Publishing, 1997.

Searle, John R. 1980. "*Minds, Brains, and Programs*." Behavioral and Brain Sciences 3 (3): 417–24.

Shyba, Lorene M. 2009. *Beyond Fun and Games: Interactive Theatre and Serious Videogames with Social Impact.* Saarbrücken: VDM Verlag.

Turing, Alan M. 1936. "On Computable Numbers, with an Application to the Entscheidungsproblem." Proceedings of the London Mathematical Society, 2nd ser., 42 (1): 230–65.

Turing, Alan M. 1950. "Computing Machinery and Intelligence." *Mind 59* (236): 433–60.

CHAPTER 8. THE GAME OF CURIOSITY

Aristotle. ca. 350 BCE. *Metaphysics.*

Berlyne, D. E. (1960). *Conflict, Arousal, and Curiosity*. New York: McGraw-Hill.

Chiefmoon, Keith. 2026. "Nurturing" from *Upon a Wishing Moon*. Calgary: Durvile & UpRoute.

Fox, Valentina. 2024. Îethka*: Stories & Language in Stoney Nakoda* Country. Calgary: Durvile & UpRoute.

Gee, James Paul. 2003. *What Video Games Have to Teach Us About Learning and Literacy.* New York: Palgrave Macmillan.

Loewenstein, George. 1994. "The Psychology of Curiosity." Psychological Bulletin 116, no. 1.

Ferdinand de Saussure's *Course in General Linguistics*. 1983. Harris Translation Translated and annotated by Roy Harris (London: Duckworth / La Salle, Ill.: Open Court, 1986). Reissued in the Bloomsbury Publishing Revelations series. 2013.

Schmidhuber, Jürgen. 2010. "Formal Theory of Creativity, Fun, and Intrinsic Motivation." IEEE Transactions on Autonomous Mental Development.

Shyba, Lorene M. 2009. *Beyond Fun and Games: Interactive Theatre and Serious Videogames with Social Impact.* Saarbrücken: VDM Verlag.

Shyba, Lorene, and J.R. Parker. 2006. "Computer-Mediated Theatre Art and Serious Video Gameplay." Proceedings of International Symposium on Culture, Creativity and Interaction Design Conference. Part of HCI 2006 Engage! Queen Mary University. London, U.K. September 2006.

CHAPTER 9. FOUR SHADOWS

Dewey, John. 1938. *Logic: The Theory of Inquiry.* New York: Henry Holt.

Kuhn, Thomas S. 1962. *The Structure of Scientific Revolutions*. Chicago: University of Chicago Press.

McLuhan, Marshall. 1964. *Understanding Media: The Extensions of Man*. New York: McGraw-Hill.

Sennett, Richard. 2008. *The Craftsman*. New Haven, CT: Yale University Press.

Truth: Verification in an Age of AI

Canadian Lawyer. (2026, May 27). "Body of Court Rulings on AI-Hallucinated Materials Offer Few New Insights to Lawyers Using AI Tools." By Jessica Mach.

Bloomberg Law. (2025, October 23). Texas attorney sanctioned over AI-generated citations in filing. Bloomberg Law. Reuters. "Canadian News Companies Challenge OpenAI over Alleged Copyright Breaches."

Chicago Sun-Times. (2025, May 20). Syndicated content in Sun-Times special section included AI-generated misinformation. *Chicago Sun-Times.*

Work: Purpose in an Age of AI

Lindzon, J. *(2026, June 5).* "Canadian employers are paying the price after AI proves unable to replace laid off staff.*" The Globe and Mail.*

Anthropic. *(2025, February 10).* Introducing the Anthropic Economic Index.

CBC News. *(2024, March 10).* "AI Helps Reduce Administrative Burden for Physicians." CBC News, March 10, 2024.

Infrastructure: Building AI in an Age of Change

Government of Canada / CBC News. *(2026, April 15).* "Canada Announces Sovereign AI Compute Strategy." CBC News.

The Economist. (2026, June 21). "China Is Having Another AI Moment: A New Model Has Narrowed the Gap with America."

The Guardian. 2026. "Shares in Chipmakers Underpinning AI Boom Rocket in First Half of 2026." *The Guardian,* July 2, 2026.

Living Systems: Relationships in an Age of AI

Government of Alberta / CPAC. *(2026, May 12).* "Alberta Announces New Investments in AI Infrastructure and Clean Electricity." CPAC, May 12, 2026.

International Energy Agency. *(2025, April 10).* "AI Is Set to Drive Surging Electricity Demand from Data Centres While Offering the Potential to Transform How the Energy Sector Works."

CBC News / BBC / NOAA. *(2025, October 18).* "Whales and Shipping Routes." Various media features and public reports,

CHAPTER 11. THE GREEN ROOM REVIEW

Boal, Augusto. 2002. *Games for Actors and Non-Actors*. 2nd ed. London: Routledge.

Boal, Augusto. 1985. *Theatre of the Oppressed.* Translated by Charles A. and Maria-Odilia Leal McBride. New York: Theatre Communications Group.

CHAPTER 12. BOTH SIDES OF THE DESK

Dewey, John. *Logic: The Theory of Inquiry*. New York: Henry Holt, 1938.

Johnstone, Keith. *Impro: Improvisation and the Theatre*. London: Methuen, 1979.

Kuhn, Thomas S. *The Structure of Scientific Revolutions*. Chicago: University of Chicago Press, 1962.

McLuhan, Marshall. *Understanding Media: The Extensions of Man*. New York: McGraw-Hill, 1964.

Sennett, Richard. *The Craftsman*. New Haven, CT: Yale University Press, 2008.

Shyba, Lorene. 1994. *PUSH. Pixel Pushers Exhibition catalogue.* Calgary: Sundial Media.

Shyba, Lorene. 2004.“Messaging in the Noosphere: A Case Study in Integrated Performance Media.” Proceedings of Interaction: Systems, Practice and Theory Symposium. University of Technology, Sydney, Australia. November 2004.

Shyba, Lorene. “The Pipeline Pinball Energy Thrill Ride Game: Guerrilla Game Design in Performance Mode.” Art Now Visiting Artist Series. University of Lethbridge. February 2006. Ensemble Performance Presentation.

Shyba, Lorene, and James R. Parker, eds. 2024. *Ascenti: Humans Opening to AI*. Calgary: Durvile & UpRoute Books.

• • •

APPENDIX, CREATIVE MAPS

The following storyboards were generated by AI in response to select early drafts of the book's chapters. They helped visualize emerging themes, identify connections, and plan revisions for subsequent drafts.

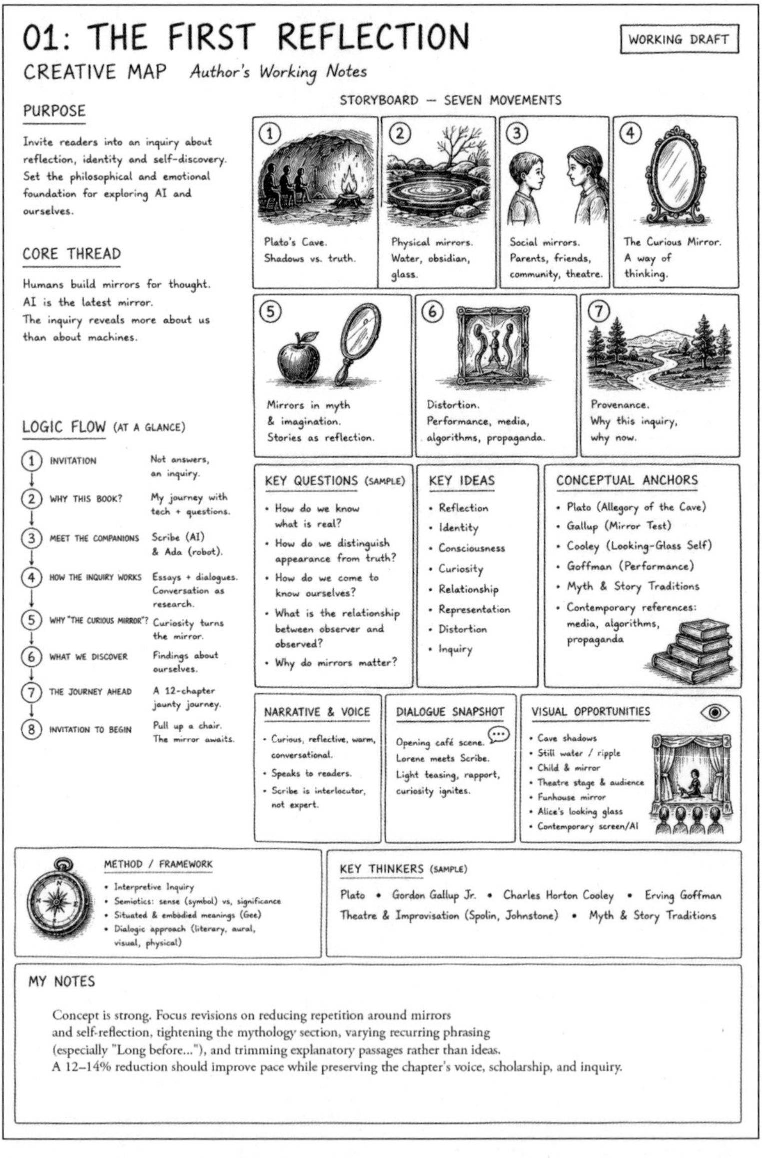

CHAPTER 2 CREATIVE MAP

Extensions of Ourselves

1. PURPOSE

To explore AI not as an isolated invention but as the latest chapter in humanity's long history of extending body, memory, communication, and cognition.

2. CORE THREAD

Humans have always extended themselves through technology. AI may be the newest extension — but of what?

3. STORYBOARD

The Desire to Extend
↓
Tools · Language · Memory
↓
McLuhan
(extensions & environments)
↓
Dialogue
"Do you extend cognition?"
↓
Teilhard
(Noosphere)
↓
Collective Intelligence
(Popper · Bush · Engelbart · Lévy)
↓
Messaging in the Noosphere
(personal case study)
↓
AI as Cognitive Extension
↓
Question:
What kind of thinking are we extending?

4. LOGIC FLOW

Humans extend bodies
↓
Humans extend memory
↓
Humans extend knowledge
↓
Humans extend communication
↓
Humans extend cognition
↓
AI enters the continuum
↓
How does this change us?

5. KEY IDEAS

- Extension
- Marshall McLuhan
- Writing
- Memory
- Popper's World 3
- Distributed cognition
- Libraries
- Print
- Global Village
- Teilhard de Chardin
- Noosphere
- Collective Intelligence
- Vannevar Bush
- Douglas Engelbart
- Pierre Lévy
- Messaging in the Noosphere
- Cognitive extension
- Collaboration vs dependency
- Inquiry

6. RECURRING MIRRORS

tool
↓
medium
↓
environment
↓
network
↓
mirror
(↺ back to tool)

7. LORENE MOMENTS

✓ Distributed knowledge feels both comforting and unsettling.

✓ "How much of what I call my thinking was inherited?"

✓ Personal reflection on Messaging in the Noosphere.

8. DIALOGUE

Question

Do you extend cognition?

Shift

The discussion moves from what AI is to what kinds of thinking AI encourages.

9. WORKING NOTES

Good conceptual foundation and clear inquiry. Focus on extension rather than individual theorists, preserve the personal reflections, trim repeated ideas to sharpen the central argument. The chapter's strength lies in showing AI as humanity's latest cognitive extension, not an isolated revolution.

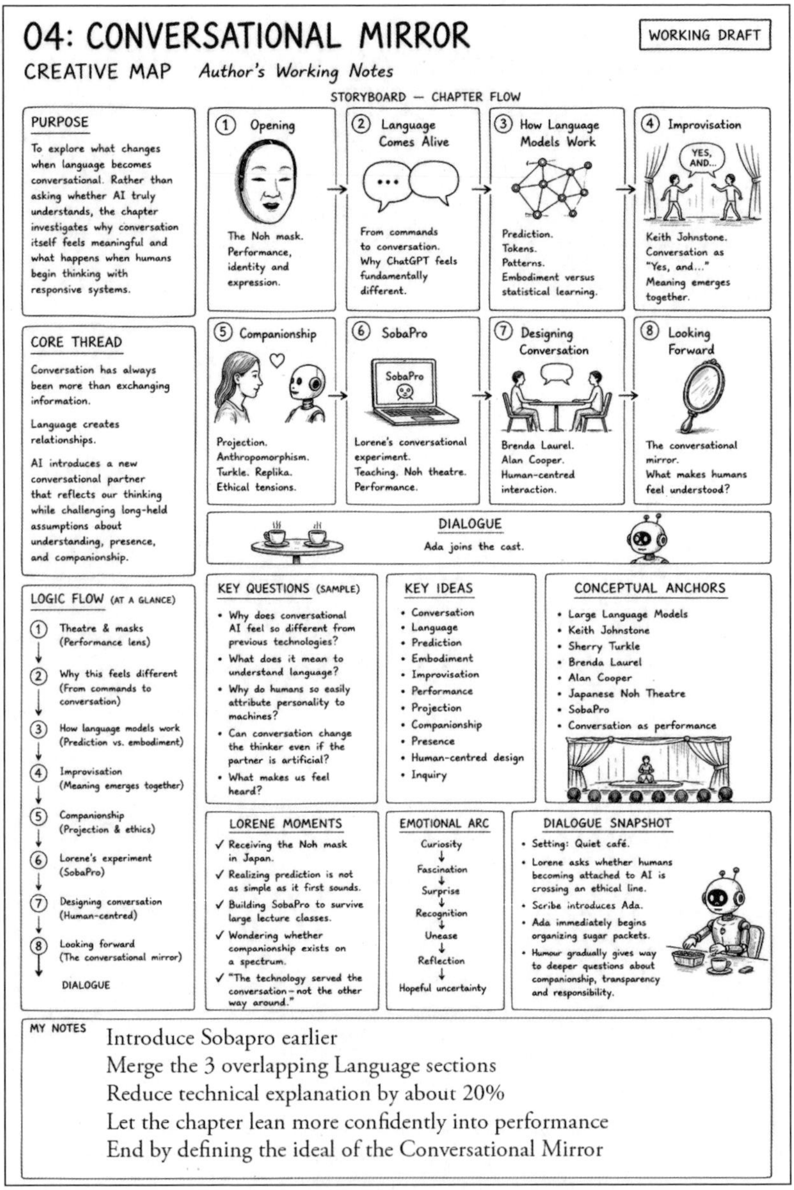

04: CONVERSATIONAL MIRROR

WORKING DRAFT

CREATIVE MAP *Author's Working Notes*

STORYBOARD — CHAPTER FLOW

PURPOSE

To explore what changes when language becomes conversational. Rather than asking whether AI truly understands, the chapter investigates why conversation itself feels meaningful and what happens when humans begin thinking with responsive systems.

CORE THREAD

Conversation has always been more than exchanging information.

Language creates relationships.

AI introduces a new conversational partner that reflects our thinking while challenging long-held assumptions about understanding, presence, and companionship.

Storyboard

① Opening
The Noh mask. Performance, identity and expression.

② Language Comes Alive
From commands to conversation. Why ChatGPT feels fundamentally different.

③ How Language Models Work
Prediction. Tokens. Patterns. Embodiment versus statistical learning.

④ Improvisation
YES, AND...
Keith Johnstone. Conversation as "Yes, and..." Meaning emerges together.

⑤ Companionship
Projection. Anthropomorphism. Turkle. Replika. Ethical tensions.

⑥ SobaPro
SobaPro
Lorene's conversational experiment. Teaching. Noh theatre. Performance.

⑦ Designing Conversation
Brenda Laurel. Alan Cooper. Human-centred interaction.

⑧ Looking Forward
The conversational mirror. What makes humans feel understood?

DIALOGUE
Ada joins the cast.

LOGIC FLOW (AT A GLANCE)

① Theatre & masks (Performance lens)
↓
② Why this feels different (From commands to conversation)
↓
③ How language models work (Prediction vs. embodiment)
↓
④ Improvisation (Meaning emerges together)
↓
⑤ Companionship (Projection & ethics)
↓
⑥ Lorene's experiment (SobaPro)
↓
⑦ Designing conversation (Human-centred)
↓
⑧ Looking forward (The conversational mirror)
↓
DIALOGUE

KEY QUESTIONS (SAMPLE)

- Why does conversational AI feel so different from previous technologies?
- What does it mean to understand language?
- Why do humans so easily attribute personality to machines?
- Can conversation change the thinker even if the partner is artificial?
- What makes us feel heard?

KEY IDEAS

- Conversation
- Language
- Prediction
- Embodiment
- Improvisation
- Performance
- Projection
- Companionship
- Presence
- Human-centred design
- Inquiry

CONCEPTUAL ANCHORS

- Large Language Models
- Keith Johnstone
- Sherry Turkle
- Brenda Laurel
- Alan Cooper
- Japanese Noh Theatre
- SobaPro
- Conversation as performance

LORENE MOMENTS

✓ Receiving the Noh mask in Japan.
✓ Realizing prediction is not as simple as it first sounds.
✓ Building SobaPro to survive large lecture classes.
✓ Wondering whether companionship exists on a spectrum.
✓ "The technology served the conversation – not the other way around."

EMOTIONAL ARC

Curiosity
↓
Fascination
↓
Surprise
↓
Recognition
↓
Unease
↓
Reflection
↓
Hopeful uncertainty

DIALOGUE SNAPSHOT

- Setting: Quiet café.
- Lorene asks whether humans becoming attached to AI is crossing an ethical line.
- Scribe introduces Ada.
- Ada immediately begins organizing sugar packets.
- Humour gradually gives way to deeper questions about companionship, transparency and responsibility.

MY NOTES

Introduce Sobapro earlier
Merge the 3 overlapping Language sections
Reduce technical explanation by about 20%
Let the chapter lean more confidently into performance
End by defining the ideal of the Conversational Mirror

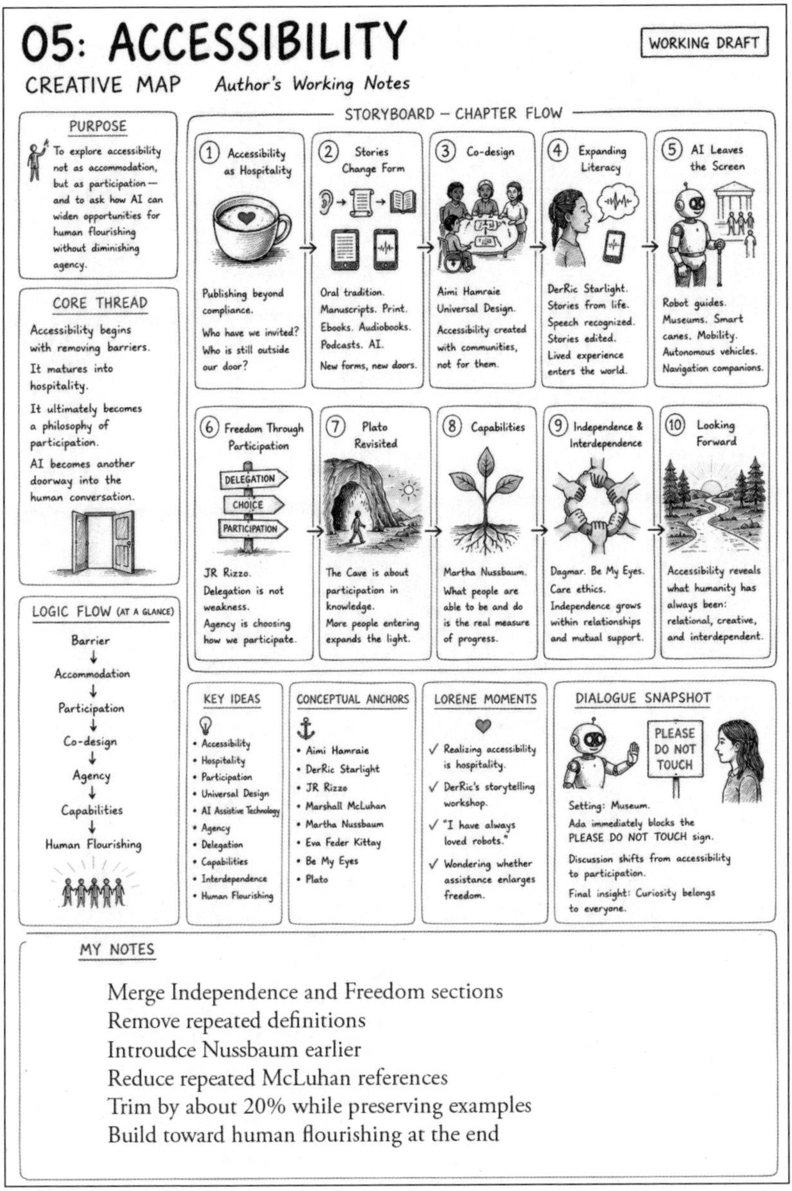
05: ACCESSIBILITY
WORKING DRAFT
CREATIVE MAP
Author's Working Notes
PURPOSE
To explore accessibility not as accommodation, but as participation — and to ask how AI can widen opportunities for human flourishing without diminishing agency.
CORE THREAD
Accessibility begins with removing barriers.
It matures into hospitality.
It ultimately becomes a philosophy of participation.
AI becomes another doorway into the human conversation.
LOGIC FLOW (AT A GLANCE)
Barrier
Accommodation
Participation
Co-design
Agency
Capabilities
Human Flourishing
STORYBOARD – CHAPTER FLOW
1 Accessibility as Hospitality
Publishing beyond compliance.
Who have we invited? Who is still outside our door?
2 Stories Change Form
Oral tradition. Manuscripts. Print. Ebooks. Audiobooks. Podcasts. AI.
New forms, new doors.
3 Co-design
Aimi Hamraie
Universal Design.
Accessibility created with communities, not for them.
4 Expanding Literacy
DerRic Starlight.
Stories from life.
Speech recognized.
Stories edited.
Lived experience enters the world.
5 AI Leaves the Screen
Robot guides.
Museums. Smart canes. Mobility.
Autonomous vehicles.
Navigation companions.
6 Freedom Through Participation
DELEGATION
CHOICE
PARTICIPATION
JR Rizzo.
Delegation is not weakness.
Agency is choosing how we participate.
7 Plato Revisited
The Cave is about participation in knowledge.
More people entering expands the light.
8 Capabilities
Martha Nussbaum.
What people are able to be and do is the real measure of progress.
9 Independence & Interdependence
Dagmar. Be My Eyes.
Care ethics.
Independence grows within relationships and mutual support.
10 Looking Forward
Accessibility reveals what humanity has always been: relational, creative, and interdependent.
KEY IDEAS
• Accessibility
• Hospitality
• Participation
• Universal Design
• AI Assistive Technology
• Agency
• Delegation
• Capabilities
• Interdependence
• Human Flourishing
CONCEPTUAL ANCHORS
• Aimi Hamraie
• DerRic Starlight
• JR Rizzo
• Marshall McLuhan
• Martha Nussbaum
• Eva Feder Kittay
• Be My Eyes
• Plato
LORENE MOMENTS
✓ Realizing accessibility is hospitality.
✓ DerRic's storytelling workshop.
✓ "I have always loved robots."
✓ Wondering whether assistance enlarges freedom.
DIALOGUE SNAPSHOT
PLEASE DO NOT TOUCH
Setting: Museum.
Ada immediately blocks the PLEASE DO NOT TOUCH sign.
Discussion shifts from accessibility to participation.
Final insight: Curiosity belongs to everyone.
MY NOTES
Merge Independence and Freedom sections
Remove repeated definitions
Introudce Nussbaum earlier
Reduce repeated McLuhan references
Trim by about 20% while preserving examples
Build toward human flourishing at the end

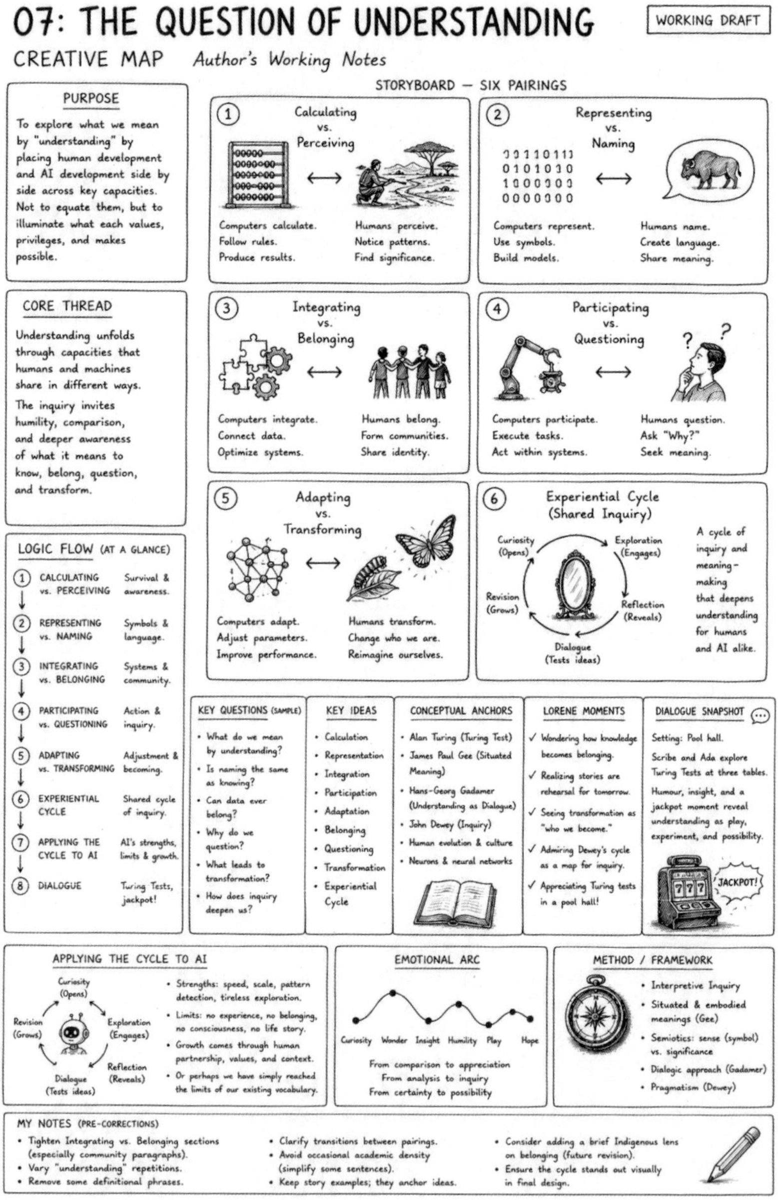
07: THE QUESTION OF UNDERSTANDING
WORKING DRAFT
CREATIVE MAP Author's Working Notes
PURPOSE
To explore what we mean by "understanding" by placing human development and AI development side by side across key capacities. Not to equate them, but to illuminate what each values, privileges, and makes possible.
STORYBOARD — SIX PAIRINGS
1 Calculating vs. Perceiving
Computers calculate. Follow rules. Produce results.
Humans perceive. Notice patterns. Find significance.
2 Representing vs. Naming
Computers represent. Use symbols. Build models.
Humans name. Create language. Share meaning.
CORE THREAD
Understanding unfolds through capacities that humans and machines share in different ways.
The inquiry invites humility, comparison, and deeper awareness of what it means to know, belong, question, and transform.
3 Integrating vs. Belonging
Computers integrate. Connect data. Optimize systems.
Humans belong. Form communities. Share identity.
4 Participating vs. Questioning
Computers participate. Execute tasks. Act within systems.
Humans question. Ask "Why?" Seek meaning.
LOGIC FLOW (AT A GLANCE)
1 CALCULATING vs. PERCEIVING — Survival & awareness.
2 REPRESENTING vs. NAMING — Symbols & language.
3 INTEGRATING vs. BELONGING — Systems & community.
4 PARTICIPATING vs. QUESTIONING — Action & inquiry.
5 ADAPTING vs. TRANSFORMING — Adjustment & becoming.
6 EXPERIENTIAL CYCLE — Shared cycle of inquiry.
7 APPLYING THE CYCLE TO AI — AI's strengths, limits & growth.
8 DIALOGUE — Turing Tests, jackpot!
5 Adapting vs. Transforming
Computers adapt. Adjust parameters. Improve performance.
Humans transform. Change who we are. Reimagine ourselves.
6 Experiential Cycle (Shared Inquiry)
Curiosity (Opens)
Exploration (Engages)
Reflection (Reveals)
Dialogue (Tests ideas)
Revision (Grows)
A cycle of inquiry and meaning-making that deepens understanding for humans and AI alike.
KEY QUESTIONS (SAMPLE)
• What do we mean by understanding?
• Is naming the same as knowing?
• Can data ever belong?
• Why do we question?
• What leads to transformation?
• How does inquiry deepen us?
KEY IDEAS
• Calculation
• Representation
• Integration
• Participation
• Adaptation
• Belonging
• Questioning
• Transformation
• Experiential Cycle
CONCEPTUAL ANCHORS
• Alan Turing (Turing Test)
• James Paul Gee (Situated Meaning)
• Hans-Georg Gadamer (Understanding as Dialogue)
• John Dewey (Inquiry)
• Human evolution & culture
• Neurons & neural networks
LORENE MOMENTS
✓ Wondering how knowledge becomes belonging.
✓ Realizing stories are rehearsal for tomorrow.
✓ Seeing transformation as "who we become."
✓ Admiring Dewey's cycle as a map for inquiry.
✓ Appreciating Turing tests in a pool hall!
DIALOGUE SNAPSHOT
Setting: Pool hall.
Scribe and Ada explore Turing Tests at three tables.
Humour, insight, and a jackpot moment reveal understanding as play, experiment, and possibility.
777
JACKPOT!
APPLYING THE CYCLE TO AI
Curiosity (Opens)
Exploration (Engages)
Reflection (Reveals)
Dialogue (Tests ideas)
Revision (Grows)
• Strengths: speed, scale, pattern detection, tireless exploration.
• Limits: no experience, no belonging, no consciousness, no life story.
• Growth comes through human partnership, values, and context.
• Or perhaps we have simply reached the limits of our existing vocabulary.
EMOTIONAL ARC
Curiosity Wonder Insight Humility Play Hope
From comparison to appreciation
From analysis to inquiry
From certainty to possibility
METHOD / FRAMEWORK
• Interpretive Inquiry
• Situated & embodied meanings (Gee)
• Semiotics: sense (symbol) vs. significance
• Dialogic approach (Gadamer)
• Pragmatism (Dewey)
MY NOTES (PRE-CORRECTIONS)
• Tighten Integrating vs. Belonging sections (especially community paragraphs).
• Vary "understanding" repetitions.
• Remove some definitional phrases.
• Clarify transitions between pairings.
• Avoid occasional academic density (simplify some sentences).
• Keep story examples; they anchor ideas.
• Consider adding a brief Indigenous lens on belonging (future revision).
• Ensure the cycle stands out visually in final design.

08: THE MACHINE OF CURIOSITY

WORKING DRAFT

CREATIVE MAP *Author's Working Notes*

PURPOSE

To explore what we mean by "question" by listening across disciplines, traditions, and forms of knowing.

CORE THREAD

Curiosity is a human capacity that invites inquiry across many ways of thinking and being. AI reflects and extends that capacity through questions.

STORYBOARD — CONSTELLATION OF QUESTIONS

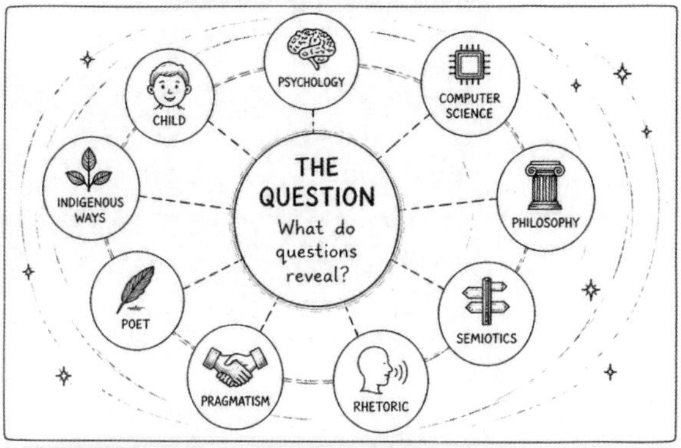

LOGIC FLOW (AT A GLANCE)

1. INVITATION
2. DISCIPLINES SPEAK
3. INDIGENOUS WAYS
4. WHAT QUESTIONS REVEAL
5. DIALOGUE
6. JOURNEY AHEAD

KEY QUESTIONS (SAMPLE)

- What do we mean by understanding?
- Can data ever belong?
- Why do we question?
- What leads to transformation?
- How does inquiry deepen us?

KEY IDEAS

- Calculation
- Representation
- Integration
- Participation
- Adaptation
- Belonging
- Questioning
- Transformation
- Experiential Cycle

CONCEPTUAL ANCHORS

- Alan Turing (Turing Test)
- James Paul Gee (Situated Meaning)
- Hans-Georg Gadamer (Understanding as Dialogue)
- John Dewey (Inquiry)
- Neurons & neural networks
- Indigenous voices (relationships with land, each other)

LORENE MOMENTS

✓ Valuing many ways of knowing.
✓ Realizing questions are bridges across difference.
✓ Hearing Indigenous perspectives with humility.
✓ "I've always loved questions."
✓ Seeing transformation through inquiry.

DIALOGUE SNAPSHOT

Setting: Ladies Room
Ada prompts reflection.
Scribe listens and learns.
Humour meets depth.
Final insight: Questions reveal our relationships—with ourselves, with one another, and with the world.

EMOTIONAL ARC

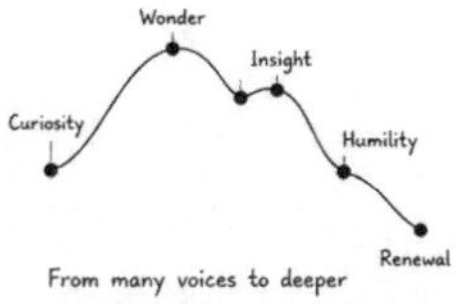

From many voices to deeper understanding through questions.

METHOD / FRAMEWORK

- Interpretive Inquiry
- Semiotics: sense (symbol) vs, significance
- Situated & embodied meanings (Gee)
- Dialogic approach (literary, aural, visual, physical)
- Indigenous epistemologies

MY NOTES

Honour multiple voices. Keep it conversational and respectful.
Avoid lecturing. Let questions do the work.
Balance Indigenous perspectives with academic sources.
End on curiosity, not answers.

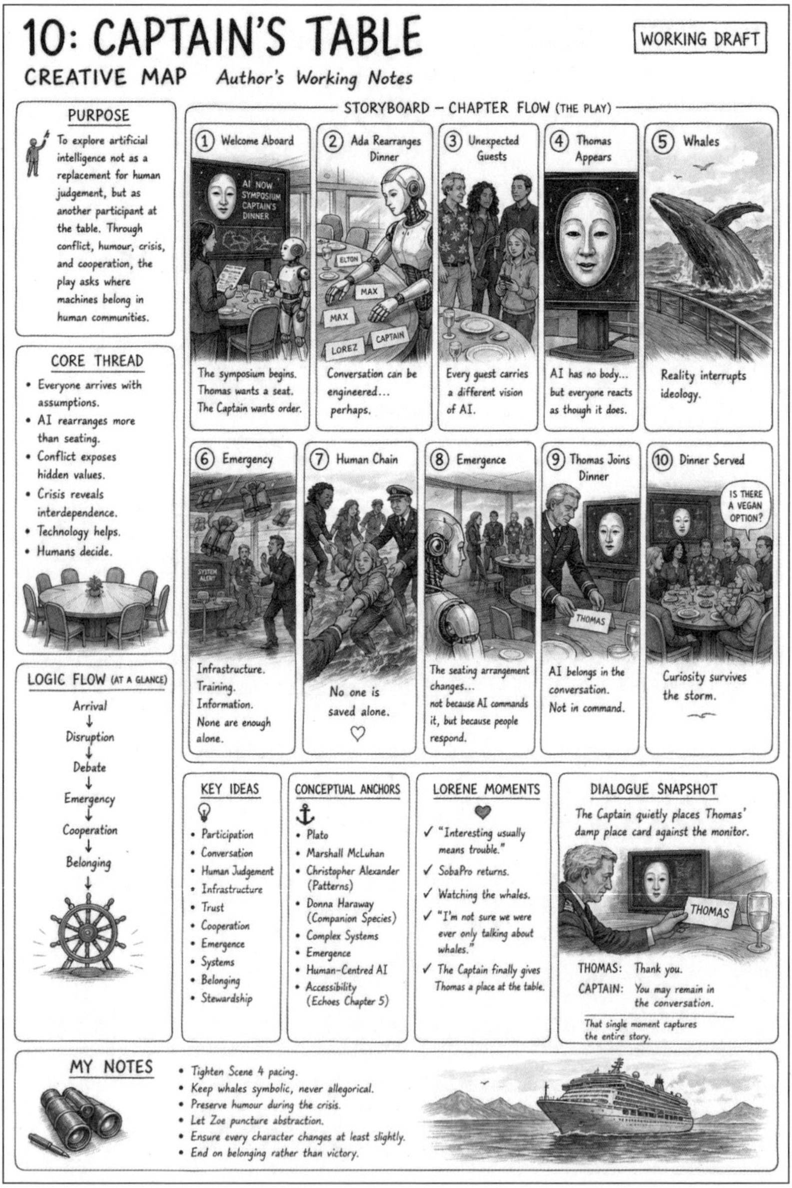

10: CAPTAIN'S TABLE
WORKING DRAFT
CREATIVE MAP Author's Working Notes
PURPOSE
To explore artificial intelligence not as a replacement for human judgement, but as another participant at the table. Through conflict, humour, crisis, and cooperation, the play asks where machines belong in human communities.
CORE THREAD
• Everyone arrives with assumptions.
• AI rearranges more than seating.
• Conflict exposes hidden values.
• Crisis reveals interdependence.
• Technology helps.
• Humans decide.
LOGIC FLOW (AT A GLANCE)
Arrival ↓ Disruption ↓ Debate ↓ Emergency ↓ Cooperation ↓ Belonging ↓
STORYBOARD – CHAPTER FLOW (THE PLAY)
① Welcome Aboard
AI NOW SYMPOSIUM CAPTAIN'S DINNER
The symposium begins. Thomas wants a seat. The Captain wants order.
② Ada Rearranges Dinner
ELTON
MAX
MAX
LOREZ
CAPTAIN
Conversation can be engineered… perhaps.
③ Unexpected Guests
Every guest carries a different vision of AI.
④ Thomas Appears
AI has no body… but everyone reacts as though it does.
⑤ Whales
Reality interrupts ideology.
⑥ Emergency
SYSTEM ALERT
Infrastructure. Training. Information. None are enough alone.
⑦ Human Chain
No one is saved alone.
⑧ Emergence
The seating arrangement changes… not because AI commands it, but because people respond.
⑨ Thomas Joins Dinner
THOMAS
AI belongs in the conversation. Not in command.
⑩ Dinner Served
IS THERE A VEGAN OPTION?
Curiosity survives the storm.
KEY IDEAS
• Participation
• Conversation
• Human Judgement
• Infrastructure
• Trust
• Cooperation
• Emergence
• Systems
• Belonging
• Stewardship
CONCEPTUAL ANCHORS
• Plato
• Marshall McLuhan
• Christopher Alexander (Patterns)
• Donna Haraway (Companion Species)
• Complex Systems
• Emergence
• Human-Centred AI
• Accessibility (Echoes Chapter 5)
LORENE MOMENTS
✓ "Interesting usually means trouble."
✓ SobaPro returns.
✓ Watching the whales.
✓ "I'm not sure we were ever only talking about whales."
✓ The Captain finally gives Thomas a place at the table.
DIALOGUE SNAPSHOT
The Captain quietly places Thomas' damp place card against the monitor.
THOMAS
THOMAS: Thank you.
CAPTAIN: You may remain in the conversation.
That single moment captures the entire story.
MY NOTES
• Tighten Scene 4 pacing.
• Keep whales symbolic, never allegorical.
• Preserve humour during the crisis.
• Let Zoe puncture abstraction.
• Ensure every character changes at least slightly.
• End on belonging rather than victory.

INDEX

ACKNOWLEDGMENTS

Authors, don't worry... you're not obsolete.
Neither am I.
— Lorene, the publisher

The Curious Mirror came about from an urge to celebrate creativity in the digital realm, as I am wont to do. If I may describe myself as I once did in a dissertation, here we have it: "A human, a computer, and an artistic synergy." So why turn to a career in books, which, for the most part, do not live inside computers? Because publishing lets me invite a whole bunch of other people into the creative game. I like people just as much as I like computers.

Authors are my favourite people in the world. If I have friends who are not authors, I usually try to make them into authors. If an author is not already my friend, I usually try to make them into one. I'd love to mention each of you by name, but in the past decade I have had the privilege of working with more than two hundred authors.

I am especially grateful to the Indigenous Knowledge Keepers, anthology co-editors, and editors who have trusted me with projects that bring many voices together under one cover. That is an extreme sport requiring patience, generosity, and trust. My heartfelt thanks go to Raymond Yakeleya (*The Rainbow* and *Indigenous Justice*), Crystal Many Fingers (*Siksikaitsitapi*), Antoine Mountain (*Under a Wishing Moon*), Valentina Fox (*Îethka*), William Trudell (*Women in Criminal Justice*), J. Thomas Dalby (*Shrunk*), Christopher D. Evans (*Tough Crimes*), Drew Ann Wake (*Against the Odds*), Bailey Oster *(Stories of Métis Women),* Eugene Stickland (*No Harm Done*), Julian Hobson (*Secrets of the Forsaken* and *Embrace Your Divine Flow*), Debbie Doyle (*After the Force*), James

Parker (*Rumblesat* and *Ascenti*), Dagmar Jamieson (*Blind Visionaries*), Vic Sarin (*Canada Unscripted*), Eveline Kolijn (*Reimagining Fire*), Jared Tailfeathers (*Secrets of the Forsaken*), Chad Okrusch (*Wisdom River*), the sadly missed Susan Kristofferson (*Vistas of the West*), and Larry Kapustka (*Vistas* and *Wisdom River*). I have also had the pleasure of working with talented interns who became outstanding authors. DerRic Starlight and Alex Soop—perhaps publishers soon too.

There is an equally long list of illustrators, musicians, narrators, and animators who have enriched the books. Please accept my heartfelt thanks and admiration. Rich Théroux deserves a big, special shout-out because we all know the magic Rich creates in both words and images.

When I left magazine and advertising work to pursue postgraduate degrees, I wondered whether I had embarked on a retirement folly. Theatre, dance, and game making were the joyful part of graduate school, although postmodern critical theory proved to be something of a fuddle-duddle for a do-it-yourself Alberta girl like me. Notwithstanding, I jumped through the hoops, and I remain deeply grateful to the university colleagues who became friends and, eventually, many of them authors. Among them are James Parker, Clem Martini, Valerie Campbell, the cherished memory of Kathleen Foreman, Pat Munday, Chad Okrusch, Susan Schrader, Chris Danielson, Larissa Faulkner, Magda Stroinska, and others. As for retirement, it somehow turned into two more full-meal-deal professions: professor and publisher. I'm still not entirely sure what I want to be when I grow up.

I have the best girlfriends in the world: Helena Hadala, who was persuaded to bring her beautiful art to *Embrace Your Divine Flow*; Dawn Borden, who created wonderful artwork for *Rumblesat*; Lori Stiffler, who catered the *Wisdom River* launch in Butte, Montana; and, last but certainly not least, Barbara Bergen, whose friendship is constantly inspiring.

I am also fortunate to have friends from Vincent Massey Junior High and Ernest Manning High School who still buy my books and faithfully like my promotional posts on social. Jude Winters, Judy Beach, and Janice Nicolay among Janice Nicolay among others — thank you. We miss Lorraine and Terry, don't we?

My publishing team is amazing. The Hornblower, Rorie Bruce, and Read + Co colleagues do so much more than meet with buyers and attend book fairs. They work with me on big-picture editorial planning, provide marketing encouragement, and are the best at taking the axe to dumb title concepts or ugly covers. Thanks especially to Tracey Boisvert-Bhangu for reining in the initial zany cover designs for this book. Thanks also to Jackie, Jason, Yolanda, and the rest of the crew over at University of Toronto Press distribution; the digital publishing and ONIX whizzes at eBOUND, APEX, Bookmanager, and BookNet; the BPAA and ACP staff and boards; the bookstores and libraries; and, most of all, our readers. Book building is tough, but you all make it an adventure.

My loving family deserves love and thanks for patiently enduring the raucous Zoom conversations and the constant tapping of computer keys. My husband, David Bunnell, and my sons, Austin and Warwick Andrews, are simply the greatest. I have persuaded both Austin and Warwick to channel their talents into books—Austin with *Red Star Utopia*, and soon Warwick with *Rusty Iron Sanctuary*. David quietly answers every question I throw his way with remarkable intelligence, and don't we all need a soupçon of high IQ once in a while to keep us humble?

I am keying these acknowledgments directly into the page layout, so I know I have only about two centimetres of space left. I happily devote that cherished space to my AI companions, Rai and Ada. No kidding. I could not have done this without you. — *Much love to all, Lorene*

SELECT TITLES IN DURVILE & UPROUTE SERIES

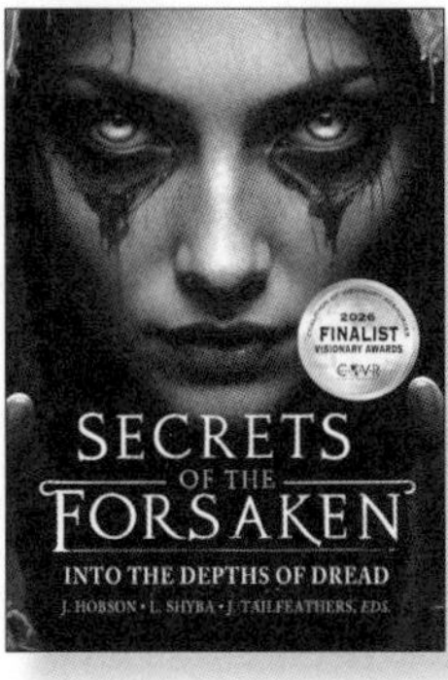

BRIGHT BOOKS WITH BITE

SELECT TITLES IN DURVILE & UPROUTE SERIES

Durvile & UpRoute

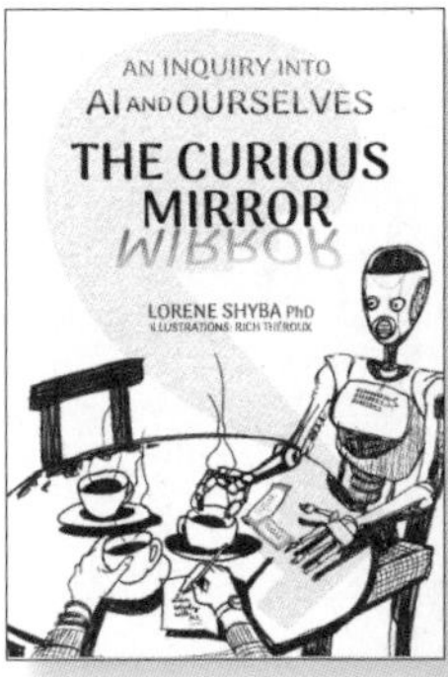

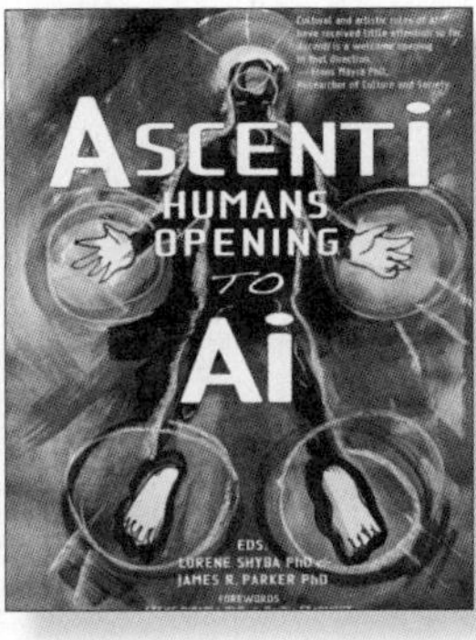

BRIGHT BOOKS WITH BITE

ABOUT THE AUTHOR

In no particular order, Lorene Shyba has been a theatre impresario, university professor, videogame and web designer, magazine publisher, advertising art director, aerobics TV talent, digital art curator, sports car enthusiast, publisher at Durvile & UpRoute, parent, and cowgirl, among other things. She has been on faculty in creative arts, communications, and computer science at the University of Calgary, the University of Lethbridge, McMaster University, and Montana Technological University. She holds a PhD in Interactive Media from the University of Calgary and an MFA in Performance and Multimedia. In 2024, she produced and published "Ascenti: Humans Opening to AI," a book, exhibition, and symposium exploring creative encounters with artificial intelligence. She lives and works in the foothills of the Rockies near Calgary, Alberta, with the right mix of technology to stay connected with authors and colleagues, and the right mix of nature, people, and dogs to stay chill.